BUILDING YOUR MARRIAGE UPON THE ROCK

THE IN-DEPTH PREMARITAL WORKBOOK WITH
THE BIBLE AS YOUR AUTHORITY AND GUIDE

Mike Williamson

Building Your Marriage Upon the Rock

Sixth printing – June 2019

© 2015 Mike Williamson

All rights reserved. No part of this material may be reproduced by any method or distributed without prior written permission from the author.

ISBN 978-0-9794715-1-3

Printed in the United States of America
Color House Graphics, Inc. Grand Rapids, MI   www.colorhousegraphics.com

Cover Design: TLC Creative Services, Inc.   www.tlccreative.com

Unless otherwise stated, all Scripture quotations are from the King James Bible translation. Archaic words may be replaced with modern usage.

Scripture quotations marked "NKJV" are taken from the New King James Version ®.
Copyright © 1982 by Thomas Nelson, Inc. Used by permission. All rights reserved.

Genesis224 is the marriage and premarital ministry of Mike & Jewel Williamson

Visit our Websites
www.premaritalworkbook.com
www.genesis224.com

The questions many premarital books ask are surface level. This book is different; it asks the important questions that truly help prepare couples for the challenges ahead. It's also a very useful resource for married couples; we use it in our marriage ministry.

Terry Hlebo, Senior Pastor
Calvary Chapel Rialto, CA

<u>Building Your Marriage Upon the Rock</u> goes much deeper than we expected and covers sensitive yet extremely important areas. We learned more about each other (and ourselves) using this book than we did the entire year we dated prior to our engagement.

Todd and Heather

I wanted a more in-depth biblical approach to marriage for couples I was marrying and found Mike's book to be exactly what I was looking for.

Dave Goyke, Sr. Pastor
Calvary Chapel Waupaca, WI

<u>Building Your Marriage Upon the Rock</u> is the most comprehensive resource I have found for premarital couples seeking to establish a biblical foundation for marriage.

Doug Snow, Sr. Pastor
Calvary Chapel S.E. Portland, OR

This book helped us to work out some difficult situations and details of our relationship that we would never have thought to talk about. It asks some very sensitive questions in the most respectful way. It is definitely the best decision we've made for our marriage.

De'Shea and Brooke

The responsibility pastors have toward couples wanting to marry is huge! This is why I'm encouraging pastors to investigate this resource. I am very happy with <u>Building Your Marriage Upon the Rock</u> and highly recommend to others.

Leonard Eurich, Executive Pastor
The Village Church Welches, Oregon

We used several premarital counseling books in past years. Unfortunately, they didn't address many of the essential issues we are concerned about in premarital counseling. This book gets right into these issues. I especially appreciate the section on Covenant.

Mark Avila, Assistant Pastor
Calvary Chapel Moreno Valley, CA

I had the honor of being the Family and Marriage Pastor for 10 years before becoming the senior pastor. We used different premarital resources throughout the years and finally found yours. We love your book.

Mike Reed, Senior Pastor
Calvary Chapel Oceanside, CA

Contents

INTRODUCTION 9
    Notes and instructions 11

YOUR FIRST MEETING 13

SECTION 1   YOUR RELATIONSHIP WITH GOD 15
    Life's origin and purpose 16
    Relationship survey 18
    Performance-based relationship 20
    Legalism or grace? 22
    Discipleship survey 25
    Spiritual beliefs survey 26
    The Holy Spirit 28
    Daily life spiritual survey 29

SECTION 2   COVENANT 33
    Blood covenant 34
    The covenant of marriage 37
    Equally yoked 43
    Life … happens 46

SECTION 3   YOUR RELATIONSHIP 49
    Getting to know you 51
    Childhood and family life 55
    Character and personality 58
    Will you be made whole? 62

SECTION 4   BECOMING ONE 67
    Bonding 68
    Compatibility 72
    Boundaries 75
    A sports-hobby prenuptial 82
    Workaholism 84
    Skeletons in the closet 87

SECTION 5   EXTENDED RELATIONSHIPS ... 89
Your family and future in-laws ... 89
Family and in-law checklist ... 90
Previous relationships ... 91
Divorced and remarrying ... 94
Stepfamilies ... 96
Stepfamily belief survey ... 97

SECTION 6   ROLES & EXPECTATIONS ... 99
Relationship expectations ... 100
Roles & responsibility ... 102
Submission ... 107
Lifestyle expectations ... 111
Holiday expectations ... 113
Family planning ... 116
Social life ... 119

SECTION 7   COMMUNICATION ... 121
Communication inventory ... 123
What's your love language? ... 125
Resolving conflicts ... 128
Conflict resolution inventory ... 130
Issues checklist ... 132

SECTION 8   LOVE ... 135

SECTION 9   FINANCES ... 145
Financial inventory ... 147

SECTION 10   SEX ... 153
Sex survey ... 154
Sexuality and problematic issues ... 157
The wedding night, honeymoon, and beyond ... 161

APPENDIX
Congratulations ... 163
Wedding statistics ... 165
Myths about cohabitation ... 166
Notes ... 172

. . . There was a marriage in Cana of Galilee, and Jesus was invited. (John 2:1–2)

INTRODUCTION

And they lived happily ever after.

The End

So ends romance novels, romance films, and fairy tales. However, once you finish the book and close the cover, or step out of the darkened theater, reality is waiting.

What does that have to do with preparing for marriage? The ideas and expectations many engaged couples have about marriage are the same as Hollywood's version: fantasyland. This workbook presents marriage preparation in the light of reality. Accomplishing this requires balance. Engagement is a joyous time, and you are eagerly looking forward to your union. Your engagement time is filled with enthusiasm, infatuation, high emotions, and high expectations. This book seeks to lift up your union and celebrate your joy while also preparing you to go the distance in the years ahead. Down the road, when feelings come and go and expectations are unmet, the skills learned in this course will serve you well.

A good, lifelong marriage doesn't just happen. It isn't a Cinderella and handsome prince story. There isn't any magic, mystery, or luck to having a lasting, satisfying marriage. The path for such a marriage is well traveled; many have walked it. It is so well marked that any couple can have an enjoyable and successful marriage if they simply follow the path.

What is the path?

Jesus said, "I am the way, the truth, and the life. No man comes to the Father [God] but through me" (John 14:6). Jesus Christ is the path. Faith in Him and obedience to Him and to the Bible is the path for a godly, lifelong marriage. Jesus called us not only to be believers but also to be disciples. We cannot follow Jesus without submitting to His discipline–without living a disciplined life. Jesus instructs us to count the cost of following Him. (See Matt. 7:21–29, 8:19–22, 10:32–42, 16:24–25; Luke 6:46–49, 14:25–35.)

In the same way, having a godly, lifelong relationship with your spouse comes at a cost. We face a multitude of circumstances in life. Some of them are pleasant, and some of them are unpleasant or extremely painful. The traditional marriage vow includes all possibilities: *in **sickness** and in health, for richer or **poorer**, for better or **worse**, until death us do part.* (The so-called negative aspects have been emphasized because we tend to overlook and avoid them.)

Your vows are not a series of sentimental phrases you say for the sake of tradition. Rather, they state the terms of the marriage covenant. They are there so you will count the cost. You are vowing, first to God and then to each other, a binding, lifelong covenant that sets in motion a complete and complex change, not only in earthly living, but also in the kingdom of God. Marriage is first a spiritual deal. Marriage *is* made in heaven (Gen. 2:24). Marriage is the binding and bonding of two people as one. It is God's deal. "What **God** has joined together let not man separate" (Mal. 2:14–16; Matt. 19:6)

Introduction

Why this workbook?

One goal of this book is to present material relevant to a broad-based audience of differing upbringings and life situations. Some workbooks take a more lighthearted approach to premarital counseling, which might work well for couples who have maintained their purity, who come from supportive, intact families, and who have well-balanced lives. This book will certainly work for them. However, it also speaks to those whose lives have been messed up by others or who, being apart from God, have made a mess of their lives.

In our premarital ministry work, we saw the need for a workbook that would delve more deeply into the many issues couples face—both in society and in the Church. I wrote this book in order to meet that need. I thought long and hard about whether one book could and should encompass all kinds of situations and issues. I didn't want to burden couples with material that did not apply to them. But based on our experience with premarital mentoring, and from conversations with pastors about the state of affairs within the church, I opted to write an all-encompassing, single resource.

Those who come to faith in Christ are called out of various states of worldliness and sinfulness. Our fallen nature and the sins and habits of the old nature don't automatically cease to exist. We still struggle with the flesh, the world, and the forces of this fallen world. And since the world is getting darker and more perverse by the day, it's no surprise that those who come to Christ have lived very sinful lives. To varying degrees, we continue to struggle with these things after we have believed and, if not dealt with and overcome, we carry them into our marriages.

In light of increasing worldliness in the church, we intend to dig deep into your personal life and your fiancé(e)'s personal life. We cover such things as childhood and family relationship issues and traumatic experiences. We explore your views of God, the authority of the Bible, your Christian walk, and topics that go by the popular names of self-acceptance, self-respect, boundaries, and other emotional-mental mindsets. We focus on character and personality issues, religious views, habits, past relationships, and histories with addictions and lingering sins.

Another goal of this study is for you to know yourself and your fiancé(e) as clearly and honestly as possible. This workbook addresses the question of whether you know yourself and your fiancé(e) well enough to be making wise, mature, and godly choices.

Moreover, we want to elevate marriage to the sacred position to which God has placed it. Even within Christianity, the view of marriage has been cheapened. Thus, we attempt to instill this sacred view of marriage into your—the premarital couple's—mindset. Lastly (although it is actually first), the goal is to elevate your thinking to the truth that, as with all of life, marriage is foremost about God's purpose, plan, and Kingdom (Mal. 2:15–16). Marriage is mission.

May God's grace, blessing, and peace be upon you as you seek to make a marriage that honors God, is enjoyable and rewarding, and that lasts a lifetime.

Mike & Jewel Williamson
June 2019

Introduction

NOTES AND INSTRUCTIONS

Sixth printing

Other than a new cover and a few minor edits, no changes have been made between this and the previous printing. Page numbering and content remains the same.

The workbook and course

We favor going through premarital preparation with a pastor, mentor couple, or a counselor. Nevertheless, this book will serve and benefit couples who choose to do premarital preparation on their own. The consensus from many is that this book is an excellent premarital resource. It covers a lot of ground and provides in-depth structure for mentors and/or couples to follow.

Mentoring

Although this book will greatly benefit couples who choose to use it on their own, most will do this course with a pastor, a counselor, or an assigned mentor couple. No matter which type, the leader's experience, marriage, and relationship to God will be an example that offers great potential for learning and growth. Mentors usually are not pastoral counselors or licensed counselors. There are times when problematic issues surface, and someone more experienced in the Word, in the Spirit, and in counseling may be suggested for further help. One of the responsibilities of mentors is to be alert for such things and to suggest appropriate help if needed. Mentors are accountable to church leadership; they are to keep your pastor or leadership informed about your relationship and your progress in the premarital course.

Doing the work
<u>**Each person is to have his or her own workbook**</u>

It is important that you do your homework alone–by yourself. At this point, we do not want you to influence or be influenced by each other's opinions and comments. After you have completed the lesson then do, indeed, discuss and compare your answers with each other. Also, discuss your answers with each other ***before*** meeting with your mentors. This will help avoid any surprises. It is also a chance for on-the-job training in communication and conflict resolution.

 Where there is an arrow such as the one shown here, stop and do what the arrow is referencing. It is important to do the work at that time, because it relates to the material that follows. You are also to look up verses that are in line with text.

The sessions

There is no set number or duration of sessions. Meetings should be scheduled to give you time to thoroughly do the homework and discuss your answers with your fiancé(e) before each session. Since the section lengths vary, you might elect to do several sections of the book at one meeting or break a section into a couple of meetings.

Sometimes the questions spark discussion that takes the session along a path away from the format. These rabbit trails often add insight and liveliness to the session. Additionally, although

Introduction

the workbook provides structure to follow, your pastor, counselor, or mentors might alter this. For example, they may have you start with a section in the middle of the book. Perhaps your mentors will require you to write out Scriptures as well as read them. They may require you to read other books, complete an inventory, watch video presentations, and attend group meetings or seminars. Thus, while this course provides a structure to follow, it is adaptable and allows for flexibility.

Using additional paper

We encourage you to use additional paper to write more lengthy answers and comments. If you do, please use the paper's margin for noting page references and question or item numbers. This will aid in matching answers with questions during your time with your mentors.

Using the rating scales

Usually the rating scale is from 1–5 with 5 being the best, most, or most agreed, etc. Rating yourself and your fiancé(e) is a subjective and, thus, an imprecise exercise. Your mood and feelings at the time will factor into your answers. In addition, you may be uncertain what the question is asking. Therefore, do not be overly concerned about being exact. A general idea of where you *might* be with any question or issue is sufficient. Your discussion times with each other and with your mentors will allow you to explain your responses more clearly.

Additional suggested resources

Our workbook is very thorough in setting forth Kingdom principles and a solid foundation on which to prepare couples for marriage, and although there are many resources for marriage, some are better than others. Since a couple can find a wealth of resources via the Internet, the resource pages of the appendix have been eliminated. The section on communication, however, does ask questions based on Gary Chapman's book *The Five Love Languages*. Therefore, it would be advantageous for you to read his book before reaching that section. A few noteworthy resources that stand the test of time and fruitfulness are mentioned below.

Books:
- *Love and Respect* by Emerson Eggerichs. A companion book to the DVD series of the same name.
- *The Smart Stepfamily* by Ron Deal. If you are forming a stepfamily—read this.
- *Love, Sex, and Lasting Relationships* by Chip Ingram

Multimedia:
- *Love and Respect* DVD series by Emerson Eggerichs. Understanding the basic and very real needs of men and women will save you a lot of miscommunication and conflict. Many churches show the DVD series, and it is available to purchase at www.loveandrespect.com
- *We Two Are One* audio series by Pastor Alistair Begg. This audio series presents the sacred, covenantal, and God-ordained nature of marriage. www.truthforlife.org

Introduction

YOUR FIRST MEETING

Before you start

(We have assumed you are using this book with a pastor or mentor(s). If you are doing this on your own as a couple, you will still benefit by answering some of the questions on this page and the next.)

During your first meeting and before launching into the workbook, we suggest you and your mentors take some time to get to know each other. Perhaps you already know each other and have a long history. On the other hand, maybe you are strangers and meeting for the first time. If the latter is the case, we suggest you spend the first part of your initial meeting getting comfortable with one another by sharing some of your history. Perhaps you will want to share such things as how you met your fiancé(e), what attracted you to each other, your moment of decision and commitment to marry, and the process of moving through the various stages of your relationship.

This will also be a perfect time for your mentors to share some of their lives with you. They might, for example, show pictures of their wedding and share how they met. If mentors have been married a long time, pictures of before and after (much after) can be fun and encouraging. Seeing wedding pictures of a couple married for thirty years can bring a lot of hope and encouragement (not to mention laugher) to a young couple.

We hope you experience a warm, friendly relationship with your mentors. We hope they will make you comfortable and at ease. What follows in this book are some very in-depth, probing questions. Answering them will require a bond of trust between you and your mentors. Moreover, some of the material might elicit a deeper bond of trust between you and your fiancé(e).

We also hope your mentors will be appropriately transparent and candid with you about their lives. Since this book asks some deeply probing questions, it is only fair that your mentors be open about their lives too. Keep in mind that they are also human. They have issues, struggles, successes, and failures. Thus, mentors should exemplify humility and gentleness. Again, your mentors have a responsibility before God and before church leadership to speak the truth in love, to submit to the Word of God, and to deal forthrightly with your relationship and issues of marriage.

Here are some questions to help transition from introductions and getting comfortable to starting the workbook.

1. Why are you taking this course? _____

   _____

   _____

   _____

2. What do you expect from this premarital course? _____

   _____

   _____

Introduction

3. Do you have any questions or concerns about this course? _____ Any anxiety? _____ Comments?
   _____
   _____
   _____
   _____
   _____

4. What would you like from your mentors? _____
   _____
   _____
   _____
   _____
   _____

5. Are you enthusiastic about participating in this course? Would you take this course if your church or pastor did not require it? Comment _____
   _____
   _____
   _____
   _____
   _____

6. This is an intense course and the homework elicits thoughtful answers. You will be required to do the homework in a whole-hearted, timely manner. Your mentors most certainly would like your enthusiastic participation in this course. Are you *enthusiastically* committed to doing this? _____

   Finally, our goal is to make this an in-depth approach to marriage preparation while, at the same time, making it an enjoyable, beneficial experience. In addition, as the subtitle indicates, our goal is to honor God by submitting to His Word as the authority for our lives.

   Now that you have had some time to become acquainted with your mentors, let's begin at the beginning: your relationship with God.

YOUR RELATIONSHIP WITH GOD

*Seek first the kingdom of God and His righteousness and
all these things will be added to you.* (Matt. 6:33)

The above Scripture is one of the cornerstones of Christian faith. God's kingdom ought to be your heart's desire and your reference point for all the issues of your life. Premarital preparation, therefore, is first about seeking God's kingdom above all else. Your personal lives and your marriage relationship will bear the fruit of your relationship with God.

It is essential to the premarital process to establish that each person has a good foundation–the elementary teachings of the faith (Heb. 6:1–2). Some do not have the elemental things of the faith operating in their lives. This could be because they are new believers, or, if not new, they are still immature in the faith (1 Cor. 3:1–2; Gal. 4:19). Some Christians show little growth in their faith because they heard and embraced a shallow, an incomplete, or a skewed gospel (Gal 1:6–7). Therefore, the appropriate place to begin this course is with your relationship to God and to Christ. This section explores those vital relationships as well as your views of creation, the Bible, the Church, and the various teachings of biblical writers.

The apostle Paul dealt with the problem of false teachers and false doctrine propagating in the church. In one form or another, these problems have existed throughout church history. In our day, we also must deal with them. What passes for Christian doctrine is often a watered-down, humanistic gospel, a market-driven and culture-driven Christianity, a mixture of pop psychology, liberalism (rebranded as Progressive Christianity), along with evangelical types of Christianity with teachers pandering to self-centeredness and a make-me-feel-good mentality.

Thus, Christians often believe a mishmash of ideas about Christ, the Bible, and Christian living. Because of this, we will touch on some preliminary things and then get into your relationship with God. We want to establish what your overall spiritual worldview is. To do so, we will go to the very beginning—the primordial issues and aspects of life and personhood. Your views on the origin of life are the starting point.

Section 1   *Your Relationship with God*

LIFE'S ORIGIN AND PURPOSE

A worldview is the sum of thoughts, opinions, beliefs, and assumptions that shape a person's mindset. It includes elements that are religious, scientific, cultural, historical, and political. A worldview is the framework—the supporting structure—of a person's beliefs. Your worldview is the window through which you view all of life. Your spiritual worldview is what we want to consider now.

Life's origin and purpose

1. Did the universe happen out of the chance interaction of matter? Briefly, explain your thoughts about how the universe began.

   _____
   _____
   _____
   _____

2. Did we get here by evolution or partial evolution? How did we get here? _____

   _____
   _____
   _____
   _____

3. Is God: (Yes/No) A life force, a principle, the collective consciousness, etc.? _____ An individual, self-existent being with intelligence, will, purpose, and "character"? _____ The maker of all things and beings—the maker of the universe and all life? _____

4. In your own words, who or what is God? _____

   _____
   _____
   _____
   _____

5. Is Jesus God come in the flesh? (Matt. 16:13–17; John 10:30–36; 20:28) Comment _____

   _____
   _____
   _____

Section 1 — Your Relationship with God

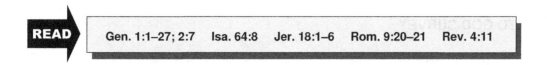

READ: Gen. 1:1–27; 2:7   Isa. 64:8   Jer. 18:1–6   Rom. 9:20–21   Rev. 4:11

Question: *What is the chief end of man?*

Answer: *To love God with all your heart, and with all your soul, and with all your mind, and with all your strength.* (Mark 12:28-3)

Man's chief end is to glorify God and to enjoy Him forever.
   The Westminster Shorter Catechism A.D. 1647

Some implications of creationism

Believing that God exists, and that He is the God of the Bible, leads to some conclusions about the essence of human life. God created us in His likeness with the attributes of consciousness, intelligence, will, emotion, desire, motive, design, purpose, and power. Discuss the following statements and be prepared to discuss them with your mentors.

1. All things that are made have design. You have been made. You have design.
2. Design means there is a designer.
3. Design means there is intelligence, intent, and purpose, which is of the designer
4. Design means that all things exist by the maker and for the maker.
5. Because you have been designed, you have a purpose.
6. Your purpose is bound up in the one who designed you–your creator.
7. You do not exist for yourself but rather for the purpose of the designer.
8. Living in conformity with the designer's intent is your life's purpose.

Example: A chair exists because of intelligence, will, and ability. A chair has design. Man designed it for himself; it exists for a purpose; it does not exist by itself or for itself. Its only purpose for existence is in the purpose of its maker (man).

6. What do you think is God's purpose for creating mankind? _____

7. What is God's purpose for creating you? _____

8. How are you fulfilling and/or cooperating with His purpose? _____

Section 1 — Your Relationship with God

RELATIONSHIP TO GOD SURVEY

| Gen. 2:7 | Deut. 8:3 | Matt. 4:4 | Matt. 7:22–23 | John 3:1–8 |
| John 4:24 | John 10:4 | John 10:14–15 | John 15:1–6 | John 17:3 |

The fundamental needs to sustain life are air, water, and food. Our foremost need is air. We can survive without food for weeks; we can survive without water for days, but we cannot survive without air for longer than a few minutes. It is interesting to note that in Genesis 2:7, God *breathed* into man the breath of life, and man became alive. We desperately need the breath of life. Similarly, in John 15:1–6, Jesus said that He is the vine, we are the branches, and that our life is desperately dependent upon remaining in Him.

What, then, is relationship to God? What does it mean? There are many varieties of religious expression. Denominational doctrines, for example, influence our views and shape our spiritual identity. They also influence our concept of God and our walk with God. Denominational affiliation, however, does not reveal much about one's actual relationship to God. Likewise, the term "born again" is often used to identify one's faith. When Jesus used the phrase, he was stating something that specifically transpires between the Spirit of God and the spirit of man. The term equates salvation to a life-giving, life-transforming, ongoing relationship.

Jesus called God His Father, and He told us to call God our Father. However, your idea of the heavenly father possibly is shaped in part by your experience with (or without) an earthly father. What thoughts and feelings do you connect with your idea of God as Father? Does it conjure up good, bad, or indifferent thoughts and feelings? Let's find out.

1. Do you have a relationship with God? _____   Do you know what this means? _____

2. What were the particulars of your salvation experience? When, where, and how were you saved? What led to your conversion? (Use additional paper or elaborate in person to your mentors.)

   _____
   _____
   _____
   _____

3. What makes you related to God? _____
   _____
   _____
   _____

4. Describe your relationship with God. _____
   _____
   _____

Section 1   *Your Relationship with God*

5. Are you born again—born of the Spirit? (John 3:3) _____ What does this mean? _____

6. Explain how God is real to you. _____

7. You can know *facts about* God through creation and through His Word. But can you **know** God, or only **know about** Him? (Matt. 7:22–23; John 10:4, 14–15; 17:3) Is there a difference? Comment

8. What does it mean to *worship* God in spirit and in truth? (John 4:24) _____

9. Check as many as apply to your views of God.
   - ☐ God is supportive and interested in me.
   - ☐ God is generally displeased with me.
   - ☐ I'm always trying to get His love.
   - ☐ I do things (even ministry) to get approval.
   - ☐ God is loving, gentle, and kind.
   - ☐ God is distant, uninvolved, unresponsive.
   - ☐ I can never satisfy Him.
   - ☐ I am never good enough.

10. Do you think of God as your: (check as many as apply)
    - ☐ Companion ☐ Lord ☐ Lover ☐ Daddy ☐ Maker
    - ☐ Friend ☐ Master ☐ Father ☐ Counselor ☐ Judge

    Other? _____

11. What is your religious–spiritual background? _____

12. How has this background influenced your life? _____

Section 1 — Your Relationship with God

PERFORMANCE-BASED RELATIONSHIP

In the movie *Pretty Woman*, the ultra-successful Edward (played by Richard Gere) stops and asks a street prostitute, Vivian, (played by Julia Roberts) for directions. Since she knows the way to Beverly Hills and can drive a stick-shift car better than he can, she takes him to his destination. Edward hires Vivian as his escort while conducting business in the area. From there, he becomes enchanted with her, has a heart makeover, and they fall in love and live "happily every after."

Beyond romance and heart changes, what is another message this story delivers? The message is attraction has much to do with appearance and performance. The point is this: Edward would not have hired her, let alone continued in the relationship with her, if she wasn't pretty and charming.

It is likely that all of us somewhat buy into this message every day of our lives. Performance and appearance have much to do with how we rate each other and how we relate to each other. Some marriage problems stem from disappointment with one's mate. Simply stated, disappointment is the failure of one person to live up to the other's hopes, expectations, and standards. The same can be true of our relationship with God. For example, when God does not meet a person's expectations—when God does not perform the way a person wants or expects Him to perform—that person might become disappointed, angry, frustrated, or depressed. She/he might blame God for not listening, for being unavailable, for being distant, uncaring, and uninvolved.

In this section, you will explore the topics of performance and grace and how those are factors in your relationship with God.

1. What is your definition of performance? _____
   _____
   _____
   _____
   _____

2. Give some examples of when you experienced acceptance based on performance. _____
   _____
   _____
   _____
   _____

Most likely it was easy to list examples of consistent performance-based situations from the world. Here are some examples if you have not already listed them.

- You rush to punch the time clock so that you will not incur dismissal.
- You would be fired if you don't do your job well.
- Social contacts drop you if you are no longer cool, hip, or on top of your game.
- You are well qualified for a position but are passed over for a younger, prettier woman.
- Your car or home will be repossessed if you fall behind on payments.

Section 1   *Your Relationship with God*

This world is a fallen world, and its value system is based almost completely on performance. We learn to operate by the world's methods early in life. In our fallen nature, we are performance-based beings. As a humorous example, other than weathermen and politicians, can you think of any people who can consistently get it wrong, mess up, fail, and still keep their jobs? Probably not! But the question to explore is whether or not, and to what extent, your marriage will be based on performance and how you will respond if the performance you expect, or that your spouse expects, is not met. The Scriptures below could seem contradictory (performance vs. grace), which is why they are used as examples to ponder.

Matt. 7:17–23	Luke 6:46	Luke 18:9–14	Rom. 3:24
Rom. 5:15–18	Rom. 6:1–16	Rom. 11:6	Gal. 2:21
Gal. 5:4	Eph. 2:8–9	Eph. 4:7	Jas. 2:20–26

3. Does God expect you to perform? _____ Do you perform in order to be accepted by God? _____

_____
_____
_____
_____

4. Does God love you based on your performance? _____ Comment _____

_____
_____
_____
_____

5. Do you perform in order to be accepted and loved by your fiancé(e)? _____ Comment _____

_____
_____
_____
_____

6. a. Are there legitimate expectations of performance for marriage partners? _____

   b. If so, what are some of them? _____

_____
_____
_____
_____

Section 1 — Your Relationship with God

LEGALISM OR GRACE?

  READ | Paul's letter to the Galatians

The book of Galatians is about grace versus legalism. Your relationship with God is based on one or the other, and which of the two you follow makes all the difference. Paul started his letters with the words *Grace and peace to you.* Grace is the message of the Bible, but somehow, we manage to get the central message of the Bible twisted around and it becomes works, works, works—legalism and performance to the max.

We are prone to legalism and performance, and in that state we are apt to become the Pharisees that Jesus warned against. Paul's letter to the Galatians is devoted to confronting this tendency. What can only be given to us as a gift is what we try to earn with good works and performance. Legalism springs from the notion that we can and that we should earn our way to heaven. It is a mindset that believes we can and we must pay God back. The truth is just the opposite. We do not have the ability (worthiness) to pay God back or to earn our way to heaven (Luke 18:9–14).

Furthermore, the self-atonement mindset is the very thing that steals our joy, because the only thing joyful about salvation is that it is an unmerited gift. Enjoying receiving a paycheck is one thing—you work hard for it, and you deserve it. It gives fulfillment to your labor. It is another thing, however, to get a check in the mail just because someone wanted to bless you. How would you like to get a gift big enough to pay off your car or mortgage? Winning the lottery can't give you the *relational* payoff that a gift can. A gift says somebody loves you. The lottery says fifty million other people were hoping to get the ticket you got. No love in that!

Well, what does this have to do with getting married? Just this: If you are ruled by legalism, your whole life is affected by it, and it will taint every relationship with a spirit of, and a demand for, performance. If your beliefs about God (and yourself) are oppressive, you will be entering your marriage with an oppressive, performance-based mindset. You will expect yourself or your spouse to satisfy an image that is impossible to accomplish. Either you are expecting your spouse to make you happy and fulfilled or you are expecting yourself to be that toward your spouse. Therefore, it is important to find out if you are a grace-filled person (a person who is living in assurance of God's love for you whether you perform well or not).

1. After reading Galatians, summarize the meaning of legalism. _____
   _____
   _____
   _____
   _____

2. After reading Galatians, summarize the meaning of grace. _____
   _____
   _____
   _____
   _____

Section 1 **Your Relationship with God**

3. Have you experienced legalism in church? _____ Give examples _____
   _____
   _____
   _____

4. How has legalism influenced your life? _____
   _____
   _____
   _____

5. Are you legalistic in your own beliefs, thought life, actions, and relationships?   Comment
   _____
   _____
   _____

6. Are you living in grace? _____ Give examples of how you live in grace. _____
   _____
   _____
   _____

7. Is grace a license to be casual regarding sin and your relationship with God? (Rom. 6:1–15)
   _____
   _____
   _____

8. How have you died to your own sins? How is the new creation in Christ living in you? (2 Cor. 5:17)
   _____
   _____
   _____

9. Growing up, did you believe that acceptance from your parents was dependent on being a good boy or girl, on what you achieved, or how well you conformed to their expectations? _____   Explain
   _____
   _____
   _____

Section 1 **Your Relationship with God**

10. What is sin? _____
_____

11. When you sin, do you try harder not to sin next time? Comment _____
_____
_____

12. What emotional/mental processes do you go through when you sin? _____
_____
_____

13. Do you really (in your every day thoughts and responses) act as if God loves you and that His love for you is not based on how well you perform? Yes/No _____   Comment _____
_____
_____

14. Has your relationship with God given you freedom from such things as chronic guilt, shame, condemnation, and self-belittling? Yes/No _____   Comment _____
_____
_____

15. Has your relationship with God given you freedom from sin, habitual sinning, entertaining sin, and addictions and ungodly habits? (Matt. 1:21) Yes/No _____   Comment _____
_____
_____

READ Mark 10:17–23   Luke 15:11–32

16. Does God love you *because* you accepted Christ? _____ Would God love you even if you did not accept Christ? _____ Is God's love for you conditional or unconditional? _____

17. Did Jesus stop loving the rich young ruler who turned away from Him? _____ In the parable of the prodigal son, did the father ever stop loving the son? _____

18. Can God love you any more than He does? _____ Can God love you any less than He does? _____

19. a. What might you do to cause God to love you more? _____
_____

    b. What might you do to cause God to love you less? _____
_____

Section 1 — Your Relationship with God

DISCIPLESHIP SURVEY

> *Then one of them, which was a lawyer, asked him a question, tempting him, and saying, Master, which is the great commandment in the law?*
>
> *Jesus said unto him, you shall love the Lord your God with all your heart, and with all your soul, and with all your mind. This is the first and great commandment. And the second is like it; you shall love your neighbor as yourself. On these two commandments hang all the law and the prophets.* (Matt. 22:35–40; Mark 12:28–31)

You just completed several pages on the difference between grace, legalism, and performance. The following pages are a survey of your day-to-day spiritual life—Bible reading, prayer, and fellowship. In light of the previous material on performance, the following surveys could easily come across as legalistic and performance based. This is not our intention.

1. What does it mean to love God with all your heart? _____

2. Do you love God? How do you express that love? _____

3. Is there a difference between loving God and being "in love" with God? _____

READ ▶ Matt. 13:1–23

4. In light of the above Scripture, what kind of Christian or "hearer" are you? How would you describe your relationship to God? What kind of "ground" are you?

   ☐ Good ground? ☐ Wayside ground? ☐ Thorny ground? ☐ Shallow ground?
   ☐ Radical, vibrant, enthused? ☐ Sunday Christian? ☐ Lukewarm?

5. Are you hungry for God, for truth, for growth, for repentance, for change? Do you hunger and thirst for righteousness? _____ (Matt. 5:6)

6. Is your Christianity merely tokenism, lip service, a Sunday deal, a convenience? _____

7. Is your faith a relationship? _____ Or a religion (a bunch of do's and don'ts)? _____

Section 1   *Your Relationship with God*

Since God is your Father and Jesus said, "I must be about my father's business" (Luke 2:49),

8. Are you passionate about your heavenly Father's business? _____

9. Or are you more passionate about your own interests? _____

> *Seek first the Kingdom of God and His righteousness and all these things will be added to you.* (Matt. 6:33)

10. a. Are His Kingdom, His agenda, His honor, and His pleasure first place in your life? _____

    b. If so explain how His Kingdom, His business, and His honor are first place. _____
_____
_____
_____

    c. If not, what *is* in first place? _____
_____
_____
_____

SPIRITUAL BELIEFS SURVEY

Finish the following sentences:

1. God is _____
_____
_____

2. My relationship to God is _____
_____
_____

3. Jesus Christ is _____
_____
_____

4. My relationship to Jesus is _____
_____

Section 1   **Your Relationship with God**

5. A Christian is _____
   _____
   _____

6. A disciple is _____
   _____
   _____

7. Discipleship means _____
   _____
   _____

8. The Bible is _____
   _____
   _____

9. Sin is _____
   _____
   _____

10. My fiancé(e) and I have differing views of the following spiritual – doctrinal matters:

    ☐ God   ☐ Bible reading   ☐ Denomination
    ☐ Jesus Christ   ☐ Prayer   ☐ Attending home groups
    ☐ The Trinity   ☐ Family devotion times   ☐ Tithing
    ☐ The Holy Spirit   ☐ Church attendance or lack of ☐ Differing doctrines
    ☐ Baptism of the Holy Spirit   ☐ Sin (what is or isn't sin)   ☐ Other _____
    ☐ Gifts of the Spirit   ☐ Where to attend church   ☐ Other _____

11. If you have different views on these matters, how are you dealing with your differences?
    _____
    _____
    _____
    _____

Section 1

Section 1 **Your Relationship with God**

THE HOLY SPIRIT

| Matt. 3:11 | Luke 24:39 | John 3:1–8 | John 4:24 | Acts 1:1–8 |
| Rom. 8:9, 14 | Rom. 15:16 | 1 Cor. 6:11 | Gal. 5:18 | Eph. 4:30 |

1. Jesus said that God is a spirit. What is a spirit? (Luke 24:39; John 4:24) _____
   _____
   _____

2. Who is the Holy Spirit? _____
   _____
   _____

3. What is your relationship to and with the Holy Spirit? _____
   _____
   _____

4. What does it mean to be led by the Spirit? (Rom. 8:14; Gal. 5:18) _____
   _____
   _____

5. Do you sense His leading? _____ His voice? _____ How do you sense His leading? Comment
   _____
   _____
   _____

6. What does it mean to be baptized in (by) the Holy Spirit? (Matt. 3:11; Acts 1:1–8) _____
   _____
   _____
   _____

Some things to consider about the Holy Spirit and being born again from above, of the Father.

- We are born of the Spirit. (John 3:1–8)
- Those who are born of the Father have His Spirit. This is what makes us His children. (Rom. 8:9)
- The Holy Spirit does the work of transforming us into mature sons and daughters of God (Rom. 15:16; 1 Cor. 6:11; Phil. 2:13). Yet we have a part to play. For example, it is our responsibility to repent, and we are not to grieve the Holy Spirit. (Matt. 4:17; Luke 13:3; Eph. 4:30)

Section 1   *Your Relationship with God*

DAILY LIFE SPIRITUAL SURVEY

As stated on previous pages, these surveys are not meant to foster guilt over a sense of poor performance or a legalistic, I-should-do-this-better mentality. Rather, they are meant to see where God, through trusting Him, will move to help you in areas that He would have you embrace in order to bring you into a mature relationship with Him. These habits or activities must be viewed through the eyes of a loving father. If you do the following things out of a sense of an "I should" mentality, you will gain nothing from your effort, and your loving Father will seem unattractive. But, if you do these things out of a sense of God's overwhelming goodness and love, you will want to draw closer to this wonderful and attractive Father.

Bible reading

1. Theoretically speaking, how important is Bible reading?

    ☐ Extremely important   ☐ Moderately important   ☐ Not very important

2. How important is Bible reading in your actual practice of spiritual disciplines?

    ☐ Extremely important   ☐ Moderately important   ☐ Not very important

3. How often do you read the Bible? _____

4. What motivates you (or doesn't motivate you) to read the Bible? _____
   _____
   _____

5. On a scale of 1–5 (5 = best or most), how much does each phrase describe a consistent element of your Bible reading?

    a. I consistently read the Bible _____ I use a Bible reading plan _____
    b. I submit to the Bible as my authority and allow it to motivate me to make changes in my thought life, habits, behavior, and relationship to others _____
    c. I talk with others about what I have read and learned _____
    d. I memorize verses _____   I do word studies _____
    e. I read the Old Testament _____   I read the New Testament _____
    f. I use commentaries _____   I use a concordance _____
    g. I use Bible dictionaries _____   I use different translations _____

6. Other than the Bible, what books (by Christian or non-Christian authors) have contributed to shaping your life? _____
   _____
   _____

7. Any comments about Bible reading? _____
   _____
   _____

Section 1   **Your Relationship with God**

Prayer life

8. Do you turn to God in prayer consistently as a matter of your inclination? _____ (Luke 18:1)

9. Do you pray for your fiancé(e)? _____ Do you pray with your fiancé(e)? _____

10. Theoretically, how important is prayer?

    ☐ Extremely important   ☐ Moderately important   ☐ Not very important

11. How important is prayer in your actual practice of spiritual disciplines?

    ☐ Extremely important   ☐ Moderately important   ☐ Not very important

12. How often do you pray alone? _____

13. How often do you pray together? _____

14. What motivates (or doesn't motivate) you to pray? _____
_____
_____
_____

15. On a scale of 1–5, rate how much each phrase describes a consistent element of your prayer life.

    a. Adoration, praise, and worship of God _____   g. Asking God for personal needs _____

    b. Pouring out your joy, enthusiasm, etc. _____   h. Pouring out sorrows, hurts, etc. _____

    c. Interceding for family and friends _____   i. Interceding for missionaries _____

    d. Interceding for neighbors _____   j. Interceding for government leaders _____

    e. Interceding for pastor and other leaders _____   k. Complaining to God _____

    f. Confession of personal sins _____   l. Thanking God for blessings _____

16. Any comments about your prayer life? _____
_____
_____
_____

Prayer tips

- Use the guidelines for praying that Jesus taught (Matt. 6:5–13; Mark 11:25–26).
- God understands you completely. Talk to God in a manner that is normal for you and genuine.
- God is not impressed with a particular style of praying. He is interested in you. Be yourself and express your real thoughts, feelings, concerns, desires, needs, weaknesses, and sins.
- Bless your fiancé(e) in your prayers. Say prayers of thanks and gratitude for him or her.
- God does not expect a perfect performance; rather, He is interested in a teachable heart.

Section 1   **Your Relationship with God**

Fellowship

17. What does Heb.10:25 say about fellowship? _____
    _____

18. Is church a building? _____ An organization? _____ A function/meeting? _____

19. What is your definition of church? _____
    _____
    _____

20. Find five verses in the New Testament that contain the word "church." Write the Scripture references below. Then, using a resource such as *Vine's Bible Dictionary* or *Strong's Concordance,* briefly explain what meaning or idea the word "church" represents.

    1. _____   2. _____   3. _____   4. _____   5. _____

    _____
    _____
    _____

21. On a scale of 1–5, how much does each phrase describe a consistent element of your fellowship?

    a. I attend meetings of the church regularly. _____ # _____ times per _____
    b. I attend a local, traditional type church. _____
    c. I attend a small group meeting within a local church. _____
    d. I attend a home church. _____
    e. I get together with other Christians just as friends and hang out together. _____
    f. I am satisfied with my level of involvement with other believers. _____
    g. I am satisfied with my fiancé(e)'s level of involvement with other believers. _____
    h. I am interested in getting more involved with a local church. _____
    i. I would like church to be more relational. _____ I would like to be more relational. _____
    j. I am satisfied to be a spectator and not involved in fellowship, church, and body life. _____

22. Will you make it a priority to be relational, more active and involved in body life? _____

23. What steps will you take to do this? _____
    _____
    _____
    _____

NOTES

COVENANT

Your view of life and your view of your relationship with your spouse will change. This is a given. Change can be a healthy sign of growth, that is, of course, if the changes are toward growing closer to the Lord and to each other. During your lifetime of living together, both of you will change. You will not just get older and slower. You will also change in your views, opinions, character, and perhaps somewhat in your personalities. Events such as having children will drastically change your inner lives and outer lifestyle. How you accept or don't accept these changes will affect your relationship positively or negatively.

This changeable aspect of life is also the basis of modern marriage and divorce, which is exemplified by Hollywood films and the lifestyles of the stars. Many marriage vows are little more than expressions of sentimental, trite feelings. And we know that feelings change. What are the foremost reasons cited for divorce? Without question, they are *incompatibility* and *irreconcilable differences*. This is all a judge needs to hear to grant a divorce. Anymore, people just assume a couple will eventually divorce. In our culture, no one is expected to live together for life, almost as if it isn't normal or healthy to do so.

Hollywood-style marriages are not built on the rock that Jesus spoke of. They are not even built upon sand. Even sand is too stable! Instead, they're built on cotton candy—mere fluff. Movie stars fall in love during a filming session and fall out of love as quickly. When the relationship isn't as fun or rewarding as it was during the engagement, the reason given is that one or the other has changed. His or her feelings for the other are no longer what they were. They have fallen out of love. The solution is to end the wilted relationship and find a fresh one—one they are sure will last forever. To a lesser degree, the same mindset is true outside of Hollywood.

> **Cracker Jack Weddings**
>
> We attended a wedding in which the groom pulled the ring out of a Cracker Jack box. At the time, this was a popular and supposedly hip thing to do. Many of the guests laughed, but within a year or so, the couple divorced.
>
> Wedding vows are covenant vows. They are not for the expression of sentimental, trite feelings. Rather, they are there for you to count the cost.
>
> Covenant vows are to be defended and kept to death.

Well, if life is so changeable—if people are so changeable—how can there be any security in a relationship? How can you be sure this person will be the person you will want to be with ten years from now? He or she might be different. The other side is also possible—you might be different. How then, can we be sure? You can do as much premarital preparation as possible by completing this course, reading books, and attending small groups and seminars. In other words, you can get as much information as possible. You can do background checks on each other. You can do a lot of inner homework on yourself. All of these things are important and advisable, yet some people have done all these things and still divorce. Conversely, there are those who have done little preparation and have had good marriages that last a lifetime. Is there something else in the equation?

There is. The answer is covenant.

Section 2 — Covenant

BLOOD COVENANT

> Gen.15:1–18   Gen. 22:1–18   Deut. 4:1–2, 12:32   Lev. 17:11   Jer. 1:12; 11:1–5
> Prov. 30:5–6   Mal. 2:13–14, 16   Matt. 24:35; 26:28   Heb. 10:1–4   Rev. 22:18–19

English translations of the Bible use the words "testament" and "covenant" interchangeably. Thus, we refer to the two major divisions of the Bible as the Old-New *Testament* or the Old-New *Covenant*. In either case, the word in the original Greek is *diatheke*—a word that connotes a unilateral decision. In other words, it is a one-way covenant that God makes with us (or more precisely a covenant between the Son and Father, which includes us). Perhaps the closest human equivalent is unconditional surrender, in which the losing side of a war does not get to negotiate any terms; it's a one-way deal. This is an important distinction, because it factors into the covenant that God makes with us. It is unequivocally on His terms. We cannot add anything to it or take anything from it. (Deut. 4:1–2, 12:32; Prov. 30:5–6; Rev. 22:18–19)

Additionally, the word "testament" does not do justice to the original idea of the word. To get the depth and power of the word, we must go to the Hebraic origin and literal meaning.

If you do not understand covenant–if you do not agree with it and how it pertains to marriage–you are not ready for marriage

Strong's Bible Dictionary says the following about two related words.

beriyth – noun Strong's #1285 beriyth (ber-eeth'); from 1262 (in the sense of cutting (like 1254)); a compact (because made by passing between pieces of flesh): . . . covenant, league.

karath – verb Strong's #3772 karath (kaw-rath'); a primitive root; to cut (off, down or asunder); by implication, to destroy or consume; specifically, to covenant (i.e. make an alliance or bargain, originally by cutting flesh and passing between the pieces).

The Bible can more accurately be called the old and new *blood covenants*. It is the record of God making covenants with man. (Gen. 15:1–18; 22:1–18) God established these covenants, and they involved sacrificing animals—the cutting of flesh and the shedding of the blood for the atoning of sins. "For the life of the flesh is in the blood, and I have given it to you upon the altar to make atonement for your souls; for it is the blood that makes atonement for the soul" (Lev. 17:11).

Animal sacrifices were symbolic. Animals could never atone for the sin of man. Jesus Christ, God's divine son, became a man and shed his own blood (His pure life) for the remission of our sin as the true and heavenly atoning sacrifice (Matt. 26:28; Heb.10:1–14). God is a covenant making, covenant keeping God. "I will watch over my word to perform it" (Jer. 1:12; 11:1–5). "Heaven and earth will pass away, but my word will never pass away" (Matt. 24:35).

What does covenant have to do with marriage?

In God's sight, marriage is covenant (Mal.2:13–14). Your covenant vow is like a compass. No matter which direction you are headed, a compass always points north. Its dependability is the only reason we use it. Next, consider a spinning toy gyroscope. No matter which way you tilt the base it is on, the gyroscope remains upright. That is what covenant is. It is the compass and gyroscope of marriage. No matter which way life turns, you remain in covenant.

This is why we place so much emphasis on character. Keeping your covenant vow has everything to do with character. If your marriage vow is not sacred to you—if you break it for ungodly reasons—you are not a man or women of your word, you do not have the character it takes, and you are not marriage material. If these words seem severe, they are intended to be. Many Christians are divorcing—still claiming to be following and obeying God. Most of them have no basis for divorcing their spouse. God hates divorce, but sin and hardness of heart might leave no other option. (Mal.2:16, Matt 19:8, 1 Cor 7:10-15).

Section 2 *Covenant*

Biblical examples of covenant

Perhaps you already know about biblical covenants, but perhaps not. Many people do not have an adequate understanding of biblical covenants and their background. Take time to do a Bible study on the following Scriptures. Diligently consider them before continuing with this section.

| Josh. 9:1–27 | Josh. 10:1–7 | 1 Sam. 18:1–4 | 1 Sam. 20:1–42 |
| 2 Sam. 9:1–13 | 2 Sam. 21:1–9 | John 17:20 | |

1. What did you glean about covenants from reading Joshua chapter 9? _____
   _____
   _____
   _____

2. What does Joshua chapter 9 tell you about making a vow foolishly or lightly without adequate knowledge of the one with whom you are entering into covenant? _____
   _____
   _____

3. What does Joshua chapter 9 tell you about keeping a vow? _____
   _____
   _____

4. What does Joshua 10:1–7 reveal about the responsibility of covenant? _____
   _____
   _____

5. What does Joshua 10:1–7 reveal about the benefits of covenant? _____
   _____
   _____

6. In 1 Samuel 18:1–4, what did Jonathan and David do? _____
   _____
   _____

7. Jonathan gave David his robe, armor, sword, bow, and belt. What did that signify?
   _____
   _____

Section 2   *Covenant*

8. In 1 Samuel 20:12–17, David and Jonathan made another covenant (or reinforced the previous one). This time Jonathan asks David to make further vows. What were Jonathan's stipulations?

9. Who was included in the covenant between Jonathan and David?

10. a. In John 17:20, how is what Jesus prayed similar to Jonathan's stipulations?

    b. Who is included in the covenant Jesus made with His Father?

11. In 2 Samuel 9:1–13, how does David fulfill his covenant with Jonathan?

12. What could Mephibosheth, the son of Jonathan, do for King David?

13. Why did Mephibosheth, the grandson of Saul (David's enemy), receive this merciful and incredibly gracious treatment from David?

14. 2 Samuel 21:1–9 depicts an event that was tied to the covenant made in Joshua 9 (several hundred years before). What does that say about God's view of covenant making and keeping.

Section 2 — Covenant

THE COVENANT OF MARRIAGE

| Gen. 1:28 | Gen. 2:18 | Gen. 2:23–24 | Amos 3:3 | Matt. 6:33 |
| Matt. 19:6 | Rom. 12:5 | 1 Cor. 12:26 | Eph. 4:25 | Eph. 5:30–32 |

Recapping what we just covered: Your relationship to God is a blood covenant relationship that God has made in Jesus Christ through His shed blood. God is a covenant keeping God. He will not break His covenant. God is faithful to His covenant. His faithfulness is our eternal security. Furthermore, God hates divorce, which is, in fact, covenant breaking. God keeps His word, and He expects us to do so.

Marriage is covenant. You will be making a covenant vow. This goes way beyond feelings of mutual attraction. It goes way beyond deciding to live together. People in the Old Testament did not enter into covenants lightly. They knew the implications, responsibilities, commitment, and consequences of covenant. The following questions deal with issues and mindsets about marriage.

Your view of marriage

1. What is marriage? _____

2. How, when, why did the institution of marriage originate? _____

3. Is marriage (Yes/No)

   A social expediency? _____   An invention of society? _____   God's design and purpose? _____

4. What event or events constitute marriage? When is a couple, in fact, "married"? _____

5. What is the purpose of marriage? _____

6. Why do you want to be married (as opposed to staying single)? _____

Section 2 *Covenant*

7. Why do you want to marry *this particular person*? _____
   _____
   _____
   _____

8. What do you expect or hope marriage will be (should be) like? _____
   _____
   _____
   _____

9. What will (or should) marriage provide? _____
   _____
   _____

10. What will marriage change? _____
    _____
    _____

11. What might you have to give up or lose by getting married? _____
    _____
    _____

12. What is the tradeoff for giving up such things? What will you get in return? _____
    _____
    _____

13. Is a person's decision to enter into marriage, and how they handle marriage, anyone else's business? (Rom. 12:5; 1 Cor. 12:26; Eph. 4:25) _____
    _____
    _____
    _____

14. Do you trust your *feelings* about each other for your decision to marry? ____ Explain ____
    _____
    _____

Section 2   *Covenant*

15. Are feelings trustworthy? Comment _____

16. **For those with prior partners**: Since you had strong romantic feelings for your previous partner(s), how do you know these same types of feelings for your fiancé(e) (or his/her feelings for you) are trustworthy? Comment _____

> **DO** — **Before continuing, read 1 Corinthians chapter 7.** Thoughtfully consider this chapter and then write your answers to question 17–26.

17. Is marriage primarily about fulfilling your need for companionship, love, meaning, purpose, and for fulfilling the same needs and desires of your spouse? Yes/No_____ Comment

18. Do you believe that life itself, and therefore marriage, was made by God and is, therefore, for God's purposes—not yours? Do you believe that marriage is first about the Kingdom of God? (Matt. 6:33)

19. Do you think single people can better serve the Lord than married people? (1 Cor. 7:32–34)

20. How will your marriage serve the Lord and the Kingdom of God? How will marrying fit or fulfill God's purpose in you for his Kingdom? _____

Section 2   ***Covenant***

21. What can you do for the Kingdom of God as a married couple that you cannot do better by remaining single? (1 Cor. 7:25–40) _____
_____
_____
_____

22. How do you know it is God's will for you to marry *anyone at all* or *at this time*? (1 Cor. 7:1–2,7–8)
_____
_____
_____
_____

23. How do you know it is God's will for you to marry *this particular person*? _____
_____
_____
_____

24. What shared vision do you and your fiancé(e) have regarding your marriage and the Kingdom of God? (Amos 3:3) _____
_____
_____
_____

25. How do you know you are ready for a lifelong commitment? _____
_____
_____
_____

26. How do you know your fiancé(e) is ready for a lifelong commitment? _____
_____
_____
_____

Section 2   *Covenant*

Your view of divorce

1. Look up the word "sacred" in a dictionary and write the first few meanings. (For a great online dictionary source, go to http://www.onelook.com. Click on the "Browse Dictionaries" link.)

   _____

   _____

   _____

   If marriage is God's deal—if it is sacred, if it is for God and by God—then it is not ours to dissolve based on our will, feelings, discomfort, or displeasure. Listed below are some common reasons people grow apart and divorce. Answer each statement *yes* or *no* as to whether you believe it would be grounds for divorce.

_____	I don't love you anymore.	_____	You're emotionally unstable.
_____	You don't love me.	_____	You've become fat, old, unkempt.
_____	My needs are not being met.	_____	I'm being neglected.
_____	You're not exciting or stimulating.	_____	You're boring in bed.
_____	We have nothing in common.	_____	You're boring out of bed.
_____	The magic has gone out of our relationship.	_____	All you want from me is sex.
_____	You don't provide the lifestyle I expect.	_____	All you want from me is a paycheck.
_____	You're not going anywhere with your life.	_____	You don't make me happy.
_____	I've found someone else.	_____	You don't respect me.

2. Find the Bible verses that support the above listed reasons for divorce and write them in the space provided.

   Write the biblical references here ↘ __

   Silly, huh? But, the point is, there isn't any biblical support for such motives. Nevertheless, many who call themselves Christians divorce for these reasons anyway. If you have been divorced, or if in the future, God forbid, you initiate divorce for any of the above or similar reasons, then know that there is no biblical basis for your choice, and you are disobeying God. So, whether you were married before or not, be certain with God, yourself, and each other that your vow, your word, and your commitment will not include any of the above escape clauses or loopholes.

3. Many couples divorce over much more serious and devastating situations, such as the examples listed below. Answer each with *yes* or *no* whether any of these would be grounds for divorce. Think realistically. Some of these can be extremely difficult and some can be unbearably abusive.

_____	Alcohol or drug addiction	_____	Refusal to work at marriage	_____	Physical abuse
_____	Child molestation	_____	Pornography addiction	_____	Sexual abuse
_____	Incarceration	_____	Abortion	_____	Mental-emotional abuse
_____	Adultery	_____	Infertility of either spouse	_____	Sex (impotence, unwilling)
_____	Gambling addiction	_____	Wandering eyes	_____	Emotional-verbal abuse
_____	Lifelong debilitating illness	_____	Jealousy, possessiveness	_____	Homosexuality/lesbianism
_____	Family neglect	_____	Overspending, charge cards		

Section 2 — Covenant

4. Does making a covenant vow **lock** you into a marriage gone sour?   Yes/No ____ Comment _____
   _____
   _____
   _____

5. Does it **lock** you into enduring abuse?[1]   Yes/No ____   Comment _____
   _____
   _____
   _____
   _____

6. Do you think there are other grounds for divorce beside adultery? _____   Do you believe that Jesus excluded all other reasons for divorce? _____ (See Matt. 5:31–32.) Comment _____
   _____
   _____
   _____
   _____

Additional thoughts

When asked why they want to marry, people often make statements such as the following: *My fiancé(e) is so loving, so caring, and so wonderful! She/he treats me so nice. She/he is so good with my kids. She/he turns my crank, makes me purr . . . or whatever.* Others give more biblically minded answers such as, *I want companionship, a mate to complete me, and I want a loving, godly relationship.*

It is natural to hope our spouse will make us purr, and we want a godly marriage, but are there other, more worthy and enduring motives? The question is, what makes *you* a fit person for someone to marry? How can you be the blessing that God would have you be to your spouse? President Kennedy's famous words come to mind. "Ask not what your country can do for you, but ask what you can do for your country." In other words, look within yourself–not your fiancé(e)–for the proper motive to marry. Again, many are looking to their fiancé(e) and seeing him or her as the reason for wanting to marry rather than to their own relationship to God and their commitment to this God-ordained covenant.

Marriage creates an environment especially suited for opportunities to become like Christ. It has been said that marriage is God's pottery wheel on which to mold you or that it's His blacksmith's forge to heat you up and hammer you into the shape He wants. Or, to put it biblically, marriage is an excellent environment and opportunity to crucify the flesh and die to self.

Again, you are setting in motion a spiritual union that will have great impact on yourselves, your future children, your extended families, and ultimately on society. What you do and how you do your marriage, *is* everybody's business. You do not live to yourselves alone. Your choices will affect many people beyond yourselves.

---

[1] *Abuse* meaning harsh, cruel, defiling treatment other than the "normal" or common day-to-day offences and irritations we all do to each other.

EQUALLY YOKED

You have explained how important your relationship to God is to you and what a relationship to God means to you. If these things are the treasures of your heart, you will want not merely to have your ideas and feelings about your faith, you will also want to share them with your spouse. You will want a companion who has the same "spark" when you talk about Jesus and His kingdom. You will want someone who is genuinely connected to Jesus—someone who *owns* Jesus for his or her self. The commands about this are found in verses such as the following:

> *Do not be unequally yoked together with unbelievers: for what fellowship has righteousness with unrighteousness? and what communion has light with darkness? And what concord has Christ with Belial? or what part has he that believes with an infidel [an unbeliever]? And what agreement has the temple of God with idols? For you are the temple of the living God; as God has said, I will dwell in them, and walk in them; and I will be their God, and they shall be my people.* (2 Cor. 6:14–18)

> *The wife is bound by the law as long as her husband lives; but if her husband dies, she is at liberty to be married to whom she will; <u>only in the Lord</u>.* (1 Cor. 7:39 emphasis added)

These verses emphatically command us to marry only within the faith.[2] Sometimes Christians are willing to compromise when selecting a husband or wife, but these verses are emphatic commands. A Christian is to marry only someone who genuinely believes in, and is submitted to, Jesus Christ and to the Bible as the Word of God and the authority over his or her life.

We know, however, that there are many shades of believers. It is incumbent upon you to marry someone who not only professes belief in Christ, but one who is truly committed and surrendered to the Lord. You must determine the genuineness and the maturity of that person's faith. Some people are willing to profess Christ simply to be married to a believer. In addition, some believers will accept an insincere or shallow profession just to dull their conscience in order to get married.

Having said that, there are vast numbers of professing Christians who do not live any differently than the world and who would wreak havoc in your life should you marry one of them. There is a lot of cheap, ruinous, pseudo faith being propagated. If you think that someone is a marriage candidate simply because he or she is a Christian, you had better reconsider. A statement often heard from Christian media is that the divorce rate among those who call themselves Christians is the same as that of non-Christians.

Furthermore, some non-Christians would be more congenial marriage partners than some Christians would be. So, if this is the case, what are you to do if a decent, non-believing person comes across your path—seeing that the pickins are so slim? Should you marry Mr. or Ms. Nice and hope for the best?

You might have a congenial relationship with an unbeliever if he or she has a mild personality and is accommodating of your faith. However, you will never be able to fellowship with your spouse in the things of God. You will most likely never go to church together, and chances are your spouse will end up resenting your religious behaviors and involvement in church activities. This person simply cannot engage in those things with you no matter how nice he or she is. It is very unwise (and dangerous to your own faith) to marry someone thinking that they will come around and become a believer. Missionary dating is a flimsy excuse and a dangerous course.

Lastly, if you willfully choose to disobey God's emphatic command, how can you expect your life and your union to be a blessing? How can you expect to be blessed? Sin carries an attendant curse . . . always.

---

[2] Although the context of 2 Cor. 6:14–18 does not specifically or exclusively apply to marrying an unbeliever, the command not to do so can be inferred or included in these verses.

Section 2   *Covenant*

1. In your words, what does it mean to be equally yoked? _____
   _____
   _____
   _____

2. Explain how you are a disciple of Jesus Christ. _____
   _____
   _____
   _____

   The following verses speak of maturity in the faith.

   > However, we speak wisdom among those who are mature, yet not the wisdom of this age, nor of the rulers of this age, who are coming to nothing. (1 Cor. 2:6)

   > Brethren, do not be children in understanding; however, in malice be babes, but in understanding be mature. (1 Cor. 14:20)

   > Therefore let us, as many as are mature, have this mind; and if in anything you think otherwise, God will reveal even this to you. (Phil. 3:15)

3. Explain how you are maturing in the faith. _____
   _____
   _____
   _____

4. Explain how you are equally yoked—not only in being believers—but also in your degree of desire and love for God. _____
   _____
   _____
   _____

> **NOTE** There is more to being spiritually compatible than just believing in Christ or having the same doctrines. Believing in Christ is a radical deal. If one of you is a "Sunday Christian" and the other is full of love for the Lord, consider this difference carefully.

5. How are you headed in the same direction spiritually—in your relation to Christ, in your devotion to Christ, and in your devotion to His people? _____
   _____
   _____
   _____

Section 2   ***Covenant***

6. How are you seeking first God's kingdom? How are you working out this command in the practical living of everyday life and your sense of God leading you? _____
_____
_____
_____

7. Man: How will you be the spiritual leader? _____
_____
_____
_____

8. Man: How will your leadership be in submission to Christ and to those who are leaders in the body? (1 Cor. 16:15–16; Heb. 13:17) _____
_____
_____
_____

9. Woman: How will you follow (submit to) your husband as unto the Lord? (Eph. 5:21–24)
_____
_____
_____
_____

10. Woman: How will you put aside your own agendas for your husband's vision—wherever the vision takes you—geographically, financially, and in lifestyle? _____
_____
_____
_____

11. What makes a couple a good match in the Lord? _____
_____
_____
_____

Section 2   *Covenant*

LIFE ... HAPPENS

Life happens! That's a statement about the uncertainty of life. We make our plans, and we hope for the best, but sometimes life . . . just happens. How you respond to an unexpected event is as important as the event itself. Your response will affect the shape of your future. How would you respond to the following situations?

1. Your spouse is laid off and can't find work in his or her field. _____

2. Your spouse will not look for work outside of his/her field. _____

3. You have overwhelming debt and lose your house, possessions, car, etc. _____

4. You are unable to conceive children. _____

5. Your spouse decides that he/she doesn't want children (or decides he/she wants children after you agreed not to have any). _____

6. One of you becomes permanently disabled or paralyzed. _____

7. For physical, medical, or mental-emotional reasons, one of you is not able to perform sexually.

8. Your spouse suffers from acute depression and uses large doses of antidepressants, which leave him/her severely dysfunctional. _____

Summing it up

Those in biblical covenant were bound for life; there was no way out of the covenant. Each member was solemnly bound by his or her vow to perform according to the terms, and if they did not do so, often the penalty was death. In the Bible, there is the saying: "God do so to me [you] and more if I [you] do not fulfill my [your] end of the covenant" (1 Sam. 3:17; 14:44; 2 Sam. 19:13; 1 Kings 2:23; 2 Kings 6:31). This saying was a direct reference to blood covenant and the dead animal used in making the covenant (Gen. 15:1–18; 22:1–13). In other words, they were saying, "May God split you in half as this dead animal if you don't keep your word!" (Or, "If God doesn't kill you, I will.") Serious stuff, huh? How does this relate to marriage? Recapping what was said before:

- Marriage is covenant making (Mal. 2:14).
- Divorce is covenant breaking (Mal. 2:13–16).
- God made the marriage covenant (Gen. 2:24; Matt. 19:6).
- God hates covenant breaking (divorce) (Mal. 2:13–16).

Covenant making included terms and repercussions (curses). Again, read 2 Samuel 21:1–9. Notice that because David had made a covenant with Jonathan, he spared Jonathan's son from being included in the death sentence. Thus, two separate covenants were being honored and kept by David. People nowadays are not put to death for divorce (covenant breaking), but there are attendant curses, so to speak. Divorce destroys families. It puts obstacles before children; it causes many of them to turn to drugs, promiscuity, and other destructive behaviors. Jesus warned against causing a child to stumble (Mark 9:42).

As you have read in 1 Samuel chapters 18 and 20, when you enter marriage covenant, all that you are becomes your spouse's. David and Jonathan swore to each other before God to be the other's protector, defender, and support in every area of life. (What's yours is mine, and what's mine is yours.) This included caring for each other's family should the other die or become incapacitated.

Being in marriage covenant includes all your spouse's successes, failures, bank accounts (debts and assets), and family. For stepfamilies, it includes your mate's ex-spouse(s), stepchildren, alimony, child support responsibilities, and even former in-laws and grandparents from previous marriages. It includes your spouse's entire well being—his or her physical, mental, and emotional health, his or her body, joys, love, devotion, pleasures, sorrows, pain, baggage, habits, issues, and behaviors. All these things become yours to embrace, to live with, to enjoy, to minister to, and to bear under and support—no matter what—no matter which way life turns. That's covenant.

NOTES

Section 3   **Your Relationship with Each Other**

YOUR RELATIONSHIP

Being in love is a wonderful and exciting experience. No matter which way it expresses itself, whether head-over-heels infatuation for someone, or a more "rational" measured approach, being in love and crossing that invisible line in your heart with someone is amazing.

Do you remember seeing or meeting your fiancé(e) for the first time? What was it like? How did you respond? Did you do a little investigating by finding out more about him or her from mutual friends? Later, did you run into this mystery person unexpectedly and have that moment where you gave each other that subtle, almost imperceptible second look? Do you remember the moment when the nudge in your heart asked, *Hmm, I wonder if this is the one?*

A few words or phrases come to my mind when thinking of these times: euphoric, heady, suppressed excitement or maybe even a facade of nonchalance when friends asked you what you thought of him. *Who? . . . Him? . . . Oh, I dunno. . . Seems like a nice guy.*

No matter how it happened, you did meet, and one thing led to another. You developed romantic feelings for each other; you began bonding and are now in the process of building a foundation for a lifetime relationship. You probably feel obligated to say you know these feelings about each other are not enough to go the distance. That's what premarital mentors want to hear, right? Right! But many people *do* have a hope that their lives could turn out like in the movies if they just meet the right person. You know, like in *Sleepless in Seattle* and *You've Got Mail*. And so, you have met Mr. or Ms. Right, and once you get through all of this business stuff, from then on it's romance, fun, adventure, and togetherness. It's love! Just ask Meg Ryan and Tom Hanks!

> **It is common for couples to give more time and consideration to planning their wedding than they do to planning their marriage.**

Well then, if love is so natural, if love just "happens" to us, why all this emphasis on preparation and premarital mentoring? After all, you're in love, and you want to be with this person for the rest of your life. Why all this work that seems so mechanical? The short answer is that Hollywood's version of love is not reality. Love and marriage in the real world are not anywhere near what we watch on the movie screen. Imagine making a movie of a typical month or year of your life or about how you met your fiancé(e). Would anyone pay to see that? Probably not. Probably pretty average, huh? Here's a secret: average is reality. Average is where it's at!

Marriage preparation is about facing reality, but this doesn't mean your marriage is destined to be boring and mundane. To the contrary, the goal of marriage preparation is to ensure that your marriage will be a lifetime of love, vitality, dear companionship, fun, intimacy, and all the uplifting things we hope for and want. Just as important, though, marriage is about weathering the storms of life together. And there will be storms—maybe even hurricanes, floods, and earthquakes. Jesus said those who build their lives on solid rock would stand through the storms (Matt. 7:24–25). It is common, however, for couples to give much more time, consideration, and money to planning their *wedding* than they do to planning their *marriage* and their life together.[1]

---

[1] See the appendix for cost statistics of a typical traditional wedding.

Section 3 — Your Relationship with Each Other

But you are seeking to do things differently, and, thus, you have come to the business of marriage preparation. As you go through this workbook, keep in mind that it is written for an audience of various age groups and life situations with manifold experiences, circumstances, and worldviews. Some of what is covered might not apply to you, but much of it will.

Many people marry with little real knowledge about their partner. Some date for a very short time (3–6 months) before marrying. There are exceptions, of course. Generally, however, six months is not enough time to know someone deeply enough to be able to make a lifetime commitment. It is not enough time to make accurate judgments about the person's character, personality, values, habits, secrets, history, and spiritual condition. Second, and more to the point, some people enter marriage with little understanding of their own self; they have issues and baggage from childhood or from previous relationships. These things inhibit a person from seeing clearly and making mature, wise choices.

When erecting a skyscraper, the builders first dig deep into the ground and construct an enormous steel and concrete foundation. Ideally, the foundation is built upon solid rock. Likewise, in these sessions we will be looking at the foundation of your relationship. It's not the glamorous and romantic qualities of your love structure that we want to consider. Rather, it's the subterranean stuff. It's the stuff that nobody sees. It's your private life.

You are extending to your mentoring couple the trust to dig around in your very private life. Why is this so important? First, it is necessary for your future spouse to know the real you as much as possible. Second, as stated before, it is necessary for *you* to know the real you. Third, many of us during dating and engagement put on our best faces. We let our fiancé(e) see only what we want him or her to see. We project an image, and we seek to protect that image. After all, isn't that what we do to catch a guy or gal? We clean up and shave. We spend an extra hour arranging our makeup and wardrobe, and we never reveal unflattering issues or traits or make unflattering noises. That's the dating scene. That's the attracting and catching scene. That's the world's way of relationships. But it is a giant pitfall. Eventually, we all make unflattering gestures and noises!

Because people want to protect their budding relationship, they are apt to overlook many little, incidental things. They might dismiss them, ignore them, or think they can work on them after they are married. Consequently, they make allowances for, and excuse or compensate for, issues and behaviors that might need a different—a more mature—approach.

We gaze admiringly at flower blossoms because, with all their color and radiance, they naturally get the attention and glory. However, the roots, stems, and leaves determine the beauty of the flower. So, dear lovebirds, while admiring the beauty and joy of your love, let's roll up our sleeves and dig into the soil of your relationship.

Section 3   Your Relationship with Each Other

(Sometimes we can over complicate things!)

GETTING TO KNOW YOU

Because of the limited space provided, feel free to use additional paper to write as much as you want. These questions and your answers to them will be fuel for discussion, learning, growth, and for enriching your relationship.

I can't marry you because you don't annoy me, which means I'm still too blindly in love with you to see how annoying you are!
(c) Nick Galifianakis Used by permission

1. How long have you known each other? _____

   When did you start dating casually?   _____

   When did you start dating seriously?   _____

   When were you engaged?   _____

2. When, where, how did you first meet each other?

   _____
   _____
   _____

3. What first attracted you to your fiancé(e)? _____

   _____
   _____
   _____

4. After your first meeting, how did you come to know each other? What was it like when you crossed over the line from friendship to commitment and love? How did you begin to be in love?

   _____
   _____
   _____

5. Describe your idea of the "ideal" marriage. _____

   _____
   _____
   _____

6. Describe your idea of the "ideal" spouse. _____

   _____
   _____

Section 3　　　　　　　　　　　　　　*Your Relationship with Each Other*

7. a. Do you believe that your fiancé(e) is the one specific person God has for you? _____
   Explain: _____
   _____
   _____

   b. If you believe this, but you or your fiancé(e) should break the engagement, what effect would this have on your belief about him or her being sent by God or being the only one for you? Comment:
   _____
   _____
   _____

8. Do you believe there are others who could potentially be a good mate? Comment _____
   _____
   _____
   _____

9. What do you think are the most important factors that make a marriage a success? _____
   _____
   _____

10. Using one word, characterize your relationship. _____

11. What thoughts does the word "marriage" bring to your mind? _____
    _____
    _____
    _____

12. List the reasons (in order of importance to you) why you want to marry your fiancé(e).

    1. _____
    2. _____
    3. _____
    4. _____
    5. _____
    6. _____
    7. _____
    8. _____

Section 3 **Your Relationship with Each Other**

13. On a scale of 1–5 (5 = best), how comfortable are you in this relationship? _____

14. Are you comfortable enough with each other to have had: (Yes/No)

    Disagreements? _____   Arguments? _____   Fights? _____   Anger? _____

15. Are you comfortable with each other when seen at your worst, emotionally and relationally? _____

16. Are you comfortable with each other when seen at your worst physically i.e., sick, unkempt, without makeup, scraggly, smelly, and having bad breath? _____

17. Have you seen each other under major stress such as job loss, work pressure, death of a friend or family member, sickness, or family conflicts? _____

18. List a few (if any) of the major stresses or crises you have gone through while dating and/or engaged.

    a. _____
    b. _____
    c. _____

19. How did you or your fiancé(e) respond to these events? _____
    _____
    _____

20. List several pleasant events/milestones in your relationship. _____
    _____
    _____

21. List several painful or unpleasant events/milestones in your relationship. _____
    _____
    _____

22. What are the strong points in your relationship? _____
    _____
    _____

23. What are the weak points in your relationship? _____
    _____
    _____

24. Have you addressed these weak points? _____ What have you done to change them? _____
    _____
    _____
    _____

Section 3   *Your Relationship with Each Other*

25. Have you ever had doubts about your relationship and pending marriage? _____ If so, explain
_____
_____
_____

26. Have you ever broken off, or given thought to breaking off, your engagement? _____ If yes, explain
_____
_____

27. Do you feel any pressure to go ahead with the wedding despite some nagging inner turmoil? _____ Any pressure from your fiancé(e), parents, in-laws, or others? _____ Are you too far along in the wedding process to postpone it? _____ Comment on any turmoil you might have.
_____
_____
_____

28. Or are you *joyfully* and *wholeheartedly* looking forward to your marriage and life together? _____

29. Are you living together? _____ Have you lived together in the past?[2] _____

30. Have you been sexually active to any extent with each other? _____ If so, for how long? _____

31. (Yes/No) Is premarital sex sin? _____ A sign of disrespect? _____ Abuse? _____

32. Is either of you pressuring the other for sex? _____ What are your boundaries for physical contact?
_____
_____
_____

READ	Ps. 86:5	Ps. 103:1–3	Matt. 5:27–28	Matt. 6:12–15
	Matt. 15:18–20	Acts 15:20	1 Cor. 6:18–20	1 Cor. 10:8
	Eph. 4:32	Eph. 5:3	1 Thess. 4:3–5	1 Jn. 1:9

    Sex outside of marriage is fornication, and it *is* sin. That statement is absurd to our sexually obsessed culture. Yet these things are clear biblical commands, and they are for our own well-being and protection. Women, more so than men it seems, suffer guilt and shame for premarital sex, and some carry that guilt into their marriage. Some of these women might develop a negative attitude about sex and, therefore, be deprived of the fulfilling sexuality God intends for them. If you have had premarital sex, now is the time for you to change your minds and behavior (to repent) and to ask for and receive forgiveness from God and from one another. Restoration of your souls and having a right attitude toward God's Word and toward each other is crucial. Your mentors should be willing to help you in these matters.

---

[2] See Myths About Cohabitation in the appendix and especially the quote by C. S. Lewis at the bottom of page 171

Section 3   *Your Relationship with Each Other*

CHILDHOOD AND FAMILY LIFE

God bless you as you continue to prepare for your lifelong union. The Bible says *His banner over me is love* (Song of Solomon 2:4). How splendid (and vital) it is to have the banner of God's love over your union.

As noted in the introduction, those who use this workbook come from diverse age groups, social, cultural, economic, and relationship backgrounds. The purpose of this section is to get a general idea of your formative years—of your childhood home life—and of events that may have a bearing on your relationship and on your views, attitudes, responses, and behaviors. Many people have had experiences that negatively affected them. Often, such experiences set them up for continued crises throughout adulthood.

A good way to begin to know each other is through the history of your relationships going back to your roots—to your childhood. Perhaps you are a couple in your forties or older; maybe you have been married before and have grown children. You might think this section is not pertinent to your situation, and you might be right. However, since many older adults are still bound by things they have never uncovered or dealt with, this section should be informative and helpful for your future together. The rabbit-trail discussions sparked by these questions can be fun and illuminating. Of course, they might also open doors that have been locked with No Trespassing signs on them for most of your life.

> Intensive counseling is not within the scope of this course or the calling of mentors in general. If you have the need, you would do well to seek additional help from those who have such a calling.

Some of these questions may seem insensitive. However, since many people have suffered hurtful lives and/or have made very damaging choices in the past, we need to address unpleasant issues that are prevalent in society and that have been experienced by many of you. Therefore, pleasant or unpleasant, let's begin to get to know each other from the ground up.

1. Was yours a (check):
   - ☐ Biological (natural) two-parent home.
   - ☐ Adopted, step-, or foster-child situation.
   - ☐ Divorced or single-parent home.
   - ☐ Parent(s) unmarried, live-in lovers.
   - ☐ Homosexual or lesbian parental situation.
   - ☐ Other? _____

2. How would you characterize your childhood?
   - ☐ Good
   - ☐ Indifferent
   - ☐ Loving
   - ☐ Bad
   - ☐ Fun
   - ☐ Chaotic
   - ☐ Nurturing
   - ☐ Abusive
   - ☐ Other _____

Answer *yes* or *no* to the following questions. (If raised by other than natural parents just replace the words *father* and *mother* with whoever was the parental figure in your childhood.

3. Were your parents alcoholics or drug users? _____

4. Did you feel loved, accepted, wanted, enjoyed, and protected? _____

5. Did your father express his love for you openly and to your satisfaction? _____

6. Was your father controlling, manipulative, a tyrant? _____ Was he indifferent to you? _____

Section 3 **Your Relationship with Each Other**

7. Was your father domineering? _____ Was he passive? _____ Was he a doormat? _____

8. Was your father physically present but emotionally and relationally distant or absent? _____

9. Was your father abusive in any way? _____ Was your mother abusive in any way? _____

10. Did your mother express her love for you openly? _____ Was she controlling, manipulative? _____

11. Was your mother moody, depressed, passive, a doormat, or a victim? _____

12. Were you raped? _____ Or sexually molested in any way (either willingly or unwillingly)? _____
    If so, by whom? _____ When? _____
    Did you receive *beneficial* help (emotional-spiritual support, validation, and/or counseling)? _____
    _____

13. Were you verbally, emotionally, or mentally abused? _____ If so, by whom? _____
    _____

14. Were you physically abused (beaten, slapped, roughly treated)? _____ If so, by whom? _____
    _____

15. How did you respond to (how did you handle or cope with) this treatment? _____
    _____
    _____

16. Characterize your father (male parental figure) _____
    _____
    _____

17. Characterize your mother (female parental figure) _____
    _____
    _____

18. Answer each item Yes or No. Do you:

    1. Expect others to respect you _____
    2. Respect yourself _____
    3. Think you are right about most issues _____
    4. Allow yourself to be put down _____
    5. Think you don't deserve better in life _____
    6. Think you are worthless _____
    7. Reject abuse and put-downs _____
    8. Believe you are mediocre _____
    9. Generally accept second best _____
    10. Think you are better than others _____
    11. Think you are more spiritually mature than most others _____
    12. Think you are more spiritually mature than your mate _____
    13. Believe other's opinions are better than yours are _____
    14. Think your ideas are better than your mate's ideas _____

Section 3 **Your Relationship with Each Other**

19. Are there any emotional ties to previous relationships—any affection, bitterness, sadness, desire for revenge, hoping he/she gets his/hers, etc.? What do you feel about previous relationship(s)?

    _____
    _____
    _____

20. (For the woman) Have you had an abortion? _____ How many? _____
    If so, how has this affected you? _____
    _____
    _____
    _____

21. (For the man) Have you suggested or talked a woman into having an abortion? _____
    If so, how has this affected you? _____
    _____
    _____
    _____

22. (For the man) Did a former wife or girlfriend have an abortion against your wishes? _____
    If so, how has this affected you? _____
    _____
    _____
    _____

If you have been raped, molested, or otherwise abused; if you have had an abortion or have talked someone into having one; or if you have had any other traumatic experience, we encourage you to consider whether you are truly set free and healed from these things. Perhaps you have not dealt with them or you think they are not an issue anymore. If that is the case, these things can surface later in your marriage and wreak havoc on your family.

It is common for people who have experienced such traumas to have underlying guilt, shame, and fear. Some mothers, for example, are not able to bond with their new baby because of guilt from a past abortion. They may believe they have no right to enjoy, to love, or to be loved by this child. Such things, and many more, plague some women, and they have no peace if these things are not taken to God and left upon the altar of divine forgiveness and healing. It is also common for such people to be unaware of, or in denial of, these things.

If this is you, we again encourage you to get help. There are those who have been through this and want to help you. Many men have been affected by childhood abuse, molestation, or by previous relationships. Often, they are just too manly to realize or admit it. For some men, the thought of exploring these things, let alone sharing them with others, is unappealing. However, there are ministries that address these issues for men as well as for women.

Section 3   Your Relationship with Each Other

CHARACTER AND PERSONALITY

Character is at the top of the list of things to consider in choosing a spouse. Considering a person's character is an extremely practical matter; there is no room for sentimental feelings or fuzzy thinking. Here is the black and white of your relationship. Your character (and your spouse's character) is the substance from which your relationship is built. Your marriage will not be any better than you are.

1. Define character _____
   _____
   _____

2. How does your character make you a fit candidate for marriage? _____
   _____
   _____

3. How does your fiancé(e)'s character make him or her fit for marriage? _____
   _____
   _____

4. Do you have what it takes to keep your word in the midst of extreme circumstances such as financial crisis, chronic sickness, physical impairment, or relational disharmony with your spouse? _____

5. Are you: Check any words that describe you and your fiancé(e).   Y = You   F = Fiancé(e)

Y	F		Y	F	
☐	☐	A visionary, planning for the future	☐	☐	Self-centered (or moderately self-centered)
☐	☐	A person who dominates conversation	☐	☐	Devoted, whole-hearted type of person
☐	☐	Led by principle	☐	☐	Led by intuition
☐	☐	Led by feelings	☐	☐	On time for appointments, call when delayed
☐	☐	A man or woman of your word	☐	☐	Slothful, procrastinator

6. What motivates you? Check any words that describe you and your fiancé(e).

Y	F		Y	F	
☐	☐	Job or career	☐	☐	Shame, guilt, fear
☐	☐	Obligation, duty, responsibility	☐	☐	Sex (hormones)
☐	☐	Relationship to God	☐	☐	Making money
☐	☐	Loneliness	☐	☐	Desire for wholeness
☐	☐	Insecurity or security	☐	☐	Desire to have children, a family
☐	☐	Sports, pastimes, vacations, pleasures	☐	☐	Other? _____

Section 3 — Your Relationship with Each Other

7. Check any of the words that are characteristic of you and your fiancé(e).

Y	F		Y	F		Y	F		Y	F	
☐	☐	Active	☐	☐	Moody	☐	☐	Generous	☐	☐	Sensitive
☐	☐	Ambitious	☐	☐	Optimistic	☐	☐	Dominating	☐	☐	Insensitive
☐	☐	Submissive	☐	☐	Passive	☐	☐	Extrovert	☐	☐	Selfish
☐	☐	Self-confident	☐	☐	Fun/humorous	☐	☐	Introvert	☐	☐	Lonely
☐	☐	Worrier	☐	☐	Controlling	☐	☐	Likable	☐	☐	Uptight
☐	☐	Gentle	☐	☐	Excitable	☐	☐	Often sad	☐	☐	Leader
☐	☐	Persistent	☐	☐	Hardworking	☐	☐	Pessimistic	☐	☐	Follower
☐	☐	Imaginative	☐	☐	Nervous	☐	☐	Thin-skinned	☐	☐	Affectionate
☐	☐	Impatient	☐	☐	Easygoing	☐	☐	Thick-skinned	☐	☐	Shy
☐	☐	Good listener	☐	☐	Frugal	☐	☐	Dependable	☐	☐	Happy
☐	☐	Impulsive	☐	☐	Stingy	☐	☐	Workaholic	☐	☐	Serious

8. Check any issues that you struggle with now or have struggled with in the past. Then check any that you see in your fiancé(e).

Y	F		Y	F		Y	F	
☐	☐	Resolving conflicts	☐	☐	Drug or alcohol use	☐	☐	Eating disorder
☐	☐	Credit or debt problems	☐	☐	Unforgiveness	☐	☐	Lying
☐	☐	Anger/rage	☐	☐	Bitterness	☐	☐	Disciplining children
☐	☐	Depression	☐	☐	Unrealistic expectations	☐	☐	Sexual frustration
☐	☐	Adultery	☐	☐	Decision making	☐	☐	Homosexuality/lesbianism
☐	☐	Childhood abuse	☐	☐	Shame, guilt, fear	☐	☐	Pornography/sexual sin
☐	☐	Verbal-emotional abuse	☐	☐	Lack of communication	☐	☐	Gambling/lottery
☐	☐	Physical abuse-abuser	☐	☐	In-law interference	☐	☐	Workaholic
☐	☐	Sexual abuse-abuser	☐	☐	Possessive/jealous	☐	☐	Other? _____
☐	☐	Selfishness	☐	☐	Time with children	☐	☐	_____

9. Do you avoid (out of fear/anxiety) confrontation and conflict? _____   Does your fiancé(e)? _____

10. Do you power your way through confrontation and conflict? _____   Does your fiancé(e)? _____

11. Do you make excuses for your bad behavior? _____ If so, explain. _____
_____
_____

12. Do you overlook or make excuses for your fiancé(e)'s bad behavior? _____ If so, explain. _____
_____
_____

Section 3   *Your Relationship with Each Other*

13. Does your fiancé(e) make excuses for his/her bad behavior? _____ If so, explain. _____
    _____
    _____

14. Do you say hurtful things to your fiancé(e)? _____ Does he/she say hurtful things to you? _____

15. a. Do you readily and sincerely confess *your* sins and wrongs and ask forgiveness when you have offended your fiancé(e)? _____

    b. Does your fiancé(e) readily and sincerely confess his/her sins and wrongs and ask forgiveness when he/she has offended you? _____

16. Do you have a tendency to: dominate conversation? _____ make most or all decisions? _____
    Does your fiancé(e): dominate conservation? _____ make most or all decisions? _____

17. Do you tend to be submissive?[3] _____ Passive? _____ Acquiescent? _____

18. Are you acquiescent because you think your fiancé(e) knows better than you do? _____

19. Do you lie? _____ Do you tell little "white" lies when it is convenient or as a way to navigate through relationships? _____ Does this describe your fiancé(e)? _____

20. Do you have concerns over any traits that your fiancé(e) displays? _____ If so, explain. _____
    _____
    _____
    _____
    _____

READ → 2 Cor. 5:17   Eph. 4:22–24

Summing it up

2 Corinthians 5:17 states "If any man is in Christ he is a new creation, old things have past away." Even so, Paul instructs us to put off the old man and put on the new man (Eph. 4:22–24). The experience of being a new creature in Christ is something we grow into. Salvation instantly changes our heavenly situation, but it does not instantly change our earthly situation. We still have memories, habitual thoughts, and emotional response patterns, and often, we must live with the results of choices we have previously made. We still must deal with all the stuff of the "old man" that we are instructed to put off. Where you are along this path of transformation will greatly determine the nature of your marriage relationship.

---

[3] Section 6 goes deeper into the issues of submission.

Section 3 Your Relationship with Each Other

Rate your mate

Circle the number that reflects your level of agreement. 5 means total agreement with the statement or it totally characterizes your fiancé(e)

Disagree ← → Agree

My fiancé(e):

	Totally Disagree	Mildly Disagree	Not Sure 50/50	Mildly Agree	Totally Agree
1. is diligent with keeping, and being on time for, appointments.	1	2	3	4	5
2. calls to let me know when he/she is going to be late.	1	2	3	4	5
3. says little witty barbs that hurt me.	1	2	3	4	5
4. is moody.	1	2	3	4	5
5. treats me as an equal and does not speak or act condescendingly.	1	2	3	4	5
6. truly seeks to connect with my thoughts and emotions.	1	2	3	4	5
7. seeks my advice about decisions, thoughts, and opinions.	1	2	3	4	5
8. puts my needs and desires ahead of hers or his.	1	2	3	4	5
9. enjoys helping me with various chores.	1	2	3	4	5
10. seeks to change me into his or her image.	1	2	3	4	5
11. seeks to love me in the way that I perceive as being love.	1	2	3	4	5
12. is intimidated by my knowledge, abilities, social contacts.	1	2	3	4	5
13. is sensitive to my feelings and sees things from my point of view.	1	2	3	4	5
14. shows me great respect both privately and publicly.	1	2	3	4	5
15. is warm, affectionate, emotionally close, and available.	1	2	3	4	5
16. talks about or relates to the opposite sex in a demeaning manner.	1	2	3	4	5
17. has wandering eyes.	1	2	3	4	5
18. is courteous.	1	2	3	4	5
19. puts me before work or other interests and activities.	1	2	3	4	5
20. has repressed anger toward others or me.	1	2	3	4	5
21. seeks to change bad habits or noteworthy things that annoy me.	1	2	3	4	5
22. uses intimidating tactics (words, actions, physical contact)	1	2	3	4	5
23. uses moodiness to manipulate and control	1	2	3	4	5
24. is understanding and sympathetic toward hormonal mood swings.	1	2	3	4	5

Section 3 — Your Relationship with Each Other

WILL YOU BE MADE WHOLE?

When Jesus saw him lying there and knew that he had been a long time in that case, he said unto him, 'Will you be made whole?' (John 5:6)

One of the things that helps keep a marriage fresh is sharing a sense of adventure in discovering each other in deeper ways as your intimacy grows. You are lavishing your attention on each other, and the excitement and enthusiasm you have for each other continues to build. This course may seem like a microscopic inspection of every nook and cranny of your lives. Delving into areas not associated with your euphoric feelings might take away some of the spontaneity, mystery, and "magic" of your adventure. But, as couples settle into marriage, the thing that stifles adventure is not the microscopic attention to details but rather the lack of such attention. There is another name for the loss of attention to detail. It's called *taking each other for granted*.

> *If you try to find intimacy with another person before achieving a sense of identity on your own, all your relationships become attempts to complete yourself.*

Once we become familiar with our spouse's emotional patterns, we are tempted to see those patterns as the real person. We settle for relating to and responding to emotional and behavioral patterns and habits rather than to a unique and interesting person. In this way, we stifle the freshness of our relationship and our enjoyment of each other.

It has been said by others that we are not human *beings* so much as we are human *becomings*. Since no one is perfect, the acceptance of each other's weaknesses and shortcomings is one of the best prescriptions for your marriage. This raises a question, however, because a great deal of marriage preparation is about ferreting out and dealing with such weaknesses. But since everyone is in need of change and improvement, what are we to do? Is there some invisible standard of progress that marks us as being whole and complete enough to attract a whole, healthy person and to maintain a whole, healthy relationship?

Les and Leslie Parrott begin lectures on relationships with the following sentence: "If you try to find intimacy with another person before achieving a sense of identity on [of] your own, all your relationships become an attempt to complete yourself." [4] Since many of us suffered childhood abuse or other traumatic experiences, which continue to affect us mentally and emotionally into adulthood, how will we ever know that we are emotionally and spiritually mature enough to make such important decisions?

The following questions will help explore whether you are entering this relationship with a mature, realistic mindset. If you find yourself identifying with some of what follows, you would do well to pursue a deeper understanding through resources and biblical counseling that deal specifically with your issues.

If you can identify with any of what follows, the question Jesus asked the sick man is for you: "Will you be made whole?"

---

[4] Les & Leslie Parrott, *Relationships* (Grand Rapids, MI: Zondervan 1998), 20.

Section 3   Your Relationship with Each Other

1. General health   ☐ Excellent   ☐ Good   ☐ Fair   ☐ Poor

2. Do you have a diagnosed medical condition? _____ What? _____

3. Describe your view of alcohol use. _____
   _____

4. Do you now have, or have you ever had, an alcohol or illegal drug use problem? _____

5. Do you use prescription drugs other than prescribed by a doctor? ____ Does your fiancé(e)? _____

6. What kind of prescriptions are you taking now? _____

7. Do you take, or have you taken, mood stabilizing/mood altering prescription drugs? ____

   If so, what kind? _____
   If so, what does your fiancé(e) think of this? _____

8. Do you have, or have you had, a psychological condition? _____ Does/did your fiancé(e)? _____

Y F		Y F		Y F	
☐ ☐	Depression	☐ ☐	MPD[5]	☐ ☐	Other _____
☐ ☐	Eating disorder	☐ ☐	Bipolar	☐ ☐	Other _____

Do you have any compulsive behaviors?

Y F		Y F		Y F	
☐ ☐	Shopping	☐ ☐	Exercise	☐ ☐	Cleaning
☐ ☐	Sleeping	☐ ☐	Eating/dieting	☐ ☐	Other _____
☐ ☐	Bathing/hand washing	☐ ☐	Sexual	☐ ☐	Other _____

9. Do you have sleep problems? _____   Do you use sleep aids? _____

10. Do you have any people in your lives who are mentors and role models? (Pastor, counselor, parent, relative, or friend?) _____ Who? _____

11. Do you derive your sense of identity (worth, security, etc.) from relationships such as family, friends, fiancé(e), or children? _____ Which relationships? _____

12. a. Do you derive your sense of identity (worth) through performance, i.e., skills, career, ambition, success, money, physical conditioning? Comment _____
    _____

    b. If not, from what do you derive your sense of identity and worth? _____
    _____

---
[5] Multiple Personality Disorder

Section 3   **Your Relationship with Each Other**

13. In order to feel good about yourself and to have a sense of worth, do you need to have or to be: (check any that apply)

    ☐ Girl/boy friend   ☐ Possessions   ☐ Sexual intimacy   ☐ Control
    ☐ Husband/wife   ☐ Purpose   ☐ Money   ☐ Talent/skill
    ☐ Good looks   ☐ Fame   ☐ Successful spouse   ☐ Good income
    ☐ Friends   ☐ Family   ☐ Successful kids   ☐ Prestige
    ☐ To be organized   ☐ Intelligence   ☐ Good job   ☐ Praise from others
    ☐ Good housekeeper   ☐ College degree   ☐ Athletic ability   ☐ Good reputation
    ☐ Good cook   ☐ Upper-class lifestyle ☐ Nice shape/physique ☐ Other _____

14. Do you believe you are incomplete without another person? _____

15. Are you looking to your spouse to heal, soothe, or take away the inner emptiness, loneliness, lack of worth, or other such things within your soul? _____

16. Do you have low self-worth? _____ If so, why? From where does it spring? _____
    _____
    _____

17. Do you get security, comfort, or stimulation from other people or your fiancé(e) needing you? _____

18. Do you think your fiancé(e) is emotionally needy? _____ Does he or she seem to drain you? _____

19. Do you have a history of failed relationships? _____ Does your fiancé(e)? _____

20. Some people end up sabotaging any healthy relationship. Do you think you may have sabotaged relationships in the past? _____ Comment _____
    _____

21. Do you have a history of choosing "losers," abusers, or people with psychological problems? _____

22. Have you ever played the role of a rescuer? _____ A caretaker? _____ A peacekeeper? _____ The scapegoat? _____ The black sheep (the problem)? _____ The family secret-keeper? _____ Other? _____

23. Does your fiancé(e) have any degree of emotional dependence upon you having to convince her or him that she or he is okay, valuable, intelligent, beautiful, or a good person, etc.? _____

24. Do you seek excessive validation and affirmation from your fiancé(e)? _____ Is it ever enough? _____

25. Do you have any compulsive habits or behaviors that you rely on to buttress your self-image, your happiness, your sense of well being, or your worth? _____ Does your fiancé(e)? _____ Explain:
    _____

Section 3 **Your Relationship with Each Other**

26. Does your fiancé(e) make up for a lack in an area of your life? _____ Which area? _____
   _____
   _____

27. Is there a difference between being lonely and wanting a companion? _____ Explain _____
   _____
   _____
   _____

28. Are you desperate to be married? _____ Is your fiancé(e)? _____

29. How much does your desire or need for sex factor into your wanting to get married?
   ☐ Not much   ☐ Moderately   ☐ A lot

30. Have you ever compromised your boundaries or standards to keep a relationship? _____

31. Is a fear of being single the rest of your life pushing you to marry? _____

32. Do you need to have children to be complete and fulfilled? _____

33. Do you need to have sex in order to be complete and fulfilled? _____

34. If you have a strong desire to have children, but find after marriage that you or your spouse is incapable of having children, how will you respond and face that situation? _____
   _____
   _____

READ → John 3:16   John 16:27   Rom. 10:11
         Eph. 2:4–5   Eph. 3:17–19   1 Pet. 1:18–19

35. Will you settle for someone because you do not think you can find any better? _____

36. Are you looking to your spouse to be the good father or mother you never had? (John 16:27) _____

37. Do you have a shame-based self-image? _____ Does your fiancé(e)? _____ (Rom. 10:11)

38. Do you believe that there is something fundamentally (at your core) wrong with you? _____

39. Do you feel you are dirty? _____ Do you feel damaged? _____ Beyond fixing? _____

40. Are you lovable? _____ Or, what are you? _____

41. Do you believe God loves you extravagantly? (John 3:16; Eph. 3:17–19; 1 Pet. 1:18–19) _____

42. Is your fiancé(e) head over heels about you? _____ Are you head over heels about your fiancé(e) _____

Section 3 **Your Relationship with Each Other**

43. Does your fiancé(e) see the real you? _____ Does anybody? _____

44. What kind of masks might you be wearing or might you have worn in the past? _____
    _____
    _____

45. Deep intimacy is risky. The fear of rejection, abandonment, condemnation, disapproval, humiliation, and other such things are all very real fears. Do you have any such fears? _____
    If so, what are they? _____
    _____
    _____

46. Such fears will make you protect your inner self. They will keep you from becoming vulnerable, and vulnerability is essential for intimacy. Will you risk vulnerability and the attendant fears? _____

47. Do you comfortably trust your entire emotional self to your fiancé(e)? _____

Who are you bringing to the altar of marriage?

When we are physically sick, we run to the doctor for a cure. But, ironically, many of us who are emotionally and spiritually troubled do not run to the doctor (God) for the cure. Instead, we run to the pusher for a fix. The pusher is anybody who, or anything that, caters to and feeds our sin and character weaknesses or that masks our problems. Additionally, we believe that our troubled or sinful self is the best we can give. Often, because of our spiritual and emotional immaturity, we are willing to settle for a sin-laden, troubled, spiritually immature mate—one who, in turn, will service our own unhealthy dependence. In short, we turn to someone who will give us our fix.

> *A son honors his father and a servant his master: if then I am a father, where is mine honor? And if I am a master, where is my fear? says the LORD of hosts unto you, O priests that despise my name. And you say, "How have we despised thy name?" You offer polluted bread upon mine altar; and you say, "How have we polluted thee?" In that you say, "The table of the LORD is contemptible." And if you offer the blind for sacrifice, is it not evil?* ***And if you offer the lame and sick, is it not evil?*** *Offer it now unto your governor; will he be pleased with you, or accept your person? Says the LORD of hosts.* (Mal. 1:6–8)

This Scripture reveals the Israelites were bringing the worst of their flocks to offer to God. They did not value God enough to give Him their best. We can glean a lesson for marriage from this.

You are coming to the altar of marriage. If you have unresolved sin, or issues from childhood or from previous relationships, these things will accompany you to the altar of marriage. If you are immature, if you have issues such as a low self-image or an inflated self-image, that is your identity. It is the offering you are bringing to the altar of marriage. It is the "you" that you are offering to God and to your mate. What kind of offering are you bringing to the altar of marriage?

48. Are you offering your spouse an emotionally and spiritually mature person? _____

49. God wants the best for you, and He gave His best for you. 1 Pet. 1:18–19 says you are worth that much to Him. Do you really believe this? _____

BECOMING ONE

Therefore, shall a man leave his father and his mother, and shall cleave unto his wife: and they shall be one flesh. (Gen. 2:24)

What does it mean to become one flesh? How do two people become one flesh? Is there a process or a method?

In the making of plywood, heat, pressure, and glue are applied to multiple layers of thinly cut wood in order to bond them into one piece of plywood. Thereafter, the once-individual pieces cannot be separated without each layer being destroyed. Since marriage is a bonding process, does it require heat and pressure to make it happen? Does each person have to give up something or sacrifice him or herself in the process of becoming one?

The process of sanctification—of becoming like Jesus—of putting off the old nature and putting on the new nature—does not happen without struggle. (See Rom. 6:6; 7:7–25; Gal.5:17; Eph. 4:22; Col. 3:9–10; 1 Pet. 2:11.) Likewise, the process of bonding with your spouse and becoming one doesn't happen without at least some struggle, conflict, and resolution.

Understanding your spouse's needs is a major key in resolving conflict and overcoming other obstacles to bonding. If you do not understand (and appreciate) the essential needs of men and women in general and of your spouse in particular, you are apt to attribute wrong motives to his or her thoughts, feelings, responses, and actions—thus hampering your oneness.

Scripture tells husbands to live with their wives in an understanding way (1 Pet. 3:7). Whatever else this might mean, it at least includes seeing things from her point of view. Men, do you seek to understand and empathize with women and with what they experience just in being female? Because women experience a vast range of things men do not experience, their perspectives on life necessarily differ from those of men. God designed women to view life differently than men do. If we men do not take the time to learn, understand, accept, and appreciate this, we will miss good relationships by a mile and not even know why.

Likewise, there are things about men that women must understand, accept, and appreciate. God designed men for the roles they are to play. Traditionally, men are the breadwinners and the protectors. It is a man's duty to work, to provide for, and to protect his family (1 Tim. 5:8).[1] The male mindset, generally speaking, is geared for roles such as the provider, the protector, the conqueror of nature, and the handyman. God designed the male with essential needs, drives, and desires that are different from those of the female. If the wife does not understand and appreciate these God-designed differences, the marriage relationship will suffer.

Marriage is the act and process of bonding two people together for life. Bonding requires both spouses to live with each other in an understanding, empathetic way. The concept of bonding raises some questions, and in the next few pages, we seek your views on them.

---

[1] Women today often experience the stress of obtaining jobs and of filling the provider role. Society changed dramatically in the 1960s. Before that time, it was generally not as necessary, nor was it expected, for women (especially mothers) to work outside the home.

Section 4 — Becoming One

BONDING

Gen. 2:23–25   Gen. 3:1–24   Mal. 2:13–16
Matt. 19:4–6   1 Cor. 7:10–11   1 Pet. 3:7

1. a. What Old Testament Scripture does Jesus quote in Matthew 19:5? _____

   b. What does that tell you about His view of the book and its author? _____
   _____
   _____

2. What does Genesis 2:23 say to you about what God intends for the general relationship between all men and women? _____
   _____
   _____

3. What does Matthew 19:6 tell you about Jesus' view of marriage? _____
   _____
   _____

4. a. In light of Genesis 2:23 and 1 Peter 3:7, how should a husband look upon and treat his wife?
   _____
   _____
   _____

   b. How should a wife look upon and treat her husband? _____
   _____
   _____
   _____

5. How did sin affect the relationship between Adam and Eve? (Gen. 3:1–24) _____
   _____
   _____
   _____

Section 4   ***Becoming One***

6. How has sin affected the general relationship between all men and women? _____

7. How has sin influenced *your* attitudes, behavior, and general relationship with the opposite gender?

8. How has sin affected *your* attitudes, behavior, and relationship with your fiancé(e)? _____

9. Genesis 2:24 specifically states that the *man* is to leave his father and mother and be joined to his wife. What does that say about the man's responsibility and role? _____

10. What does God mean when He says "one flesh"? (Gen. 2:24) _____

11. How is it that God does the joining–how is marriage God's deal—if we (you) do the choosing either to marry or not to marry? _____

12. What does Jesus mean, "What therefore God has joined together, let not man separate"? (Matt. 19:6).

13. In Malachi 2:16, what does God say about divorce? _____

14. What does 1 Corinthians 7:10–11 say about divorce? _____

Section 4   **Becoming One**

15. a. Does each person lose something in the process of becoming one? _____
_____
_____

    b. If so, what do they gain? _____
_____
_____

16. Does bonding mean that you hold nothing of yourself back? Explain _____
_____
_____
_____

17. What are the differences between a couple who live together and/or are sexually involved and a couple who marry? _____
_____
_____

18. Since marriage is only for this life, why go through all the fuss—the headache, pain, sorrow, care, and concern of bonding—to become one flesh? One of you might die in the middle of raising a family. Why, then, put your heart out there for such a tenuous thing? Why put your whole self into it? It's like the lyrics of a once-popular song: *Who needs a heart when a heart can be broken?* [2] Comment
_____
_____
_____

19. Would you be incomplete without *this* person? _____ Do you need a mate in order to be or feel complete? _____

20. Some people, although married for many years, have never bonded. Why do you suppose that is?
_____
_____

21. Do you have any fears of bonding? _____ Do you think your fiancé(e) does? _____ Which ones?

      You   ☐ Emotionally   ☐ Physically/Sexually   ☐ Spiritually   ☐ As a family
      Your fiancé(e)   ☐ Emotionally   ☐ Physically/Sexually   ☐ Spiritually   ☐ As a family

---
[2] *What's Love Got to Do with It?* Terry Britten and Graham Lyle. Performed by Tina Turner 1984.

Section 4   **Becoming One**

Bonding inhibitors and promoters

22. Check any of these that might inhibit you from bonding with your mate, and then check the ones that you think might inhibit your mate from bonding with you. Y = You, F = Fiancé(e)

Y	F		Y	F	
☐	☐	Childhood abuse or other traumas	☐	☐	Emotional ties to previous relationships
☐	☐	Childhood relationships – single parent, etc.	☐	☐	A wandering eye—a flirtatious spirit
☐	☐	Broken trust in previous relationships	☐	☐	Your mate doesn't value you above others
☐	☐	Reticence to put all your eggs in one basket	☐	☐	Over involvement of parents or in-laws
☐	☐	Comparing yourself or your mate with others	☐	☐	Obsessive hobbies, work, ministry
☐	☐	Withholding the real you for fear of rejection	☐	☐	Super-spiritual or sub-spiritual mindset.

23. List other things that would inhibit you from bonding. _____
_____
_____

24. List things that encourage, stimulate, and promote bonding. _____
_____
_____
_____

25. Could fear of relinquishing or losing control have some connection with a failure to bond?
_____
_____
_____

26. Explain how bonding is, in fact, happening and to your satisfaction. _____
_____
_____
_____
_____

27. If you are not satisfied with the level of bonding, what will you do about it? _____
_____
_____
_____

COMPATIBILITY

Much has been written about compatibility. Dating services and Web sites abound that offer matchmaking based on finding a compatible partner. People seek compatible partners to marry, and people divorce because they are incompatible. So then, what in the world is compatibility? What does it have to do with living together, having a wonderful marriage, and being faithful through thick and thin?

Do you think of a compatible partner as someone who shares similar interest and values? Is it someone with the looks that you like, or the voice, the talents, the whatever? Is a compatible partner one who complements you in almost every way and doesn't hassle you or rub you the wrong way? If that's your idea of compatibility, you will be disappointed! We are individual personalities. Our many nuances and quirks make that idealistic definition of compatibility impossible. You can certainly find someone who enjoys the same sports, hobbies, and other pursuits as you do. You can find someone with the looks that please you, and, of course, you want someone whose personality is appealing to you. All of this does have an influence on your attraction to each other, and if this is compatibility, fine. But what do you do when your wonderful lovebird starts acting like an old crow? In the final analysis, compatibility has more to do with cutting each other a lot of slack—a huge amount of slack! Or, to put it biblically:

> *When you pray, forgive, if you have anything against another so that your Father also who is in heaven may forgive you your trespasses. But if you do not forgive, neither will your Father who is in heaven forgive your trespasses.* (Mark 11:25–26)
>
> *Forbearing one another, and forgiving one another, if any man has a quarrel against another, even as Christ forgave you, so also you must [forgive].* (Col. 3:13)

Opposites attract. It's a saying that people more or less accept simply because it is so common and so often quoted. But is it true? Regarding sexual attraction, yes, it's true. However, in seeking a marriage partner, we should want some common interests and many common values, not opposing ones. This type of compatibility *is* important, and you want to agree about many issues–both major and minor. Compatibility is especially important in your spiritual union, which is addressed in another section.

Compatibility is also a major factor when it comes to unspoken rules and unspoken roles that each person brings into a marriage. It's safe to say that your families of origin do many things differently. For example, they might not agree on all issues, celebrate holidays the same way, or handle money similarly. Each family has unique rules, roles, and atmospheres. Throughout childhood, your family's rules and roles were naturally instilled into your own life pattern. Problems can occur in your relationship with your spouse simply because you assume these rules and roles are the way every family should work. When your spouse does something to break those unspoken rules, conflicts either emerge or lurk in the background and remain unresolved, perhaps for years. The cure for such things is to bring them out in the open, to discuss them, and then to negotiate and develop a new set of rules and roles explicitly for *your* union.

Many of us do, it seems, marry our opposite in personality and temperament. It is commonly believed that we see in the other person a desirable trait that we think is lacking in us. For example, a passive, noncompetitive person may be attracted to an ambitious, competitive person. A fun-loving, outgoing person might marry someone with a quiet, sober temperament. Whatever the case or explanation regarding our personality match up, these types of compatibility can only take us so far. After that, something greater (such as spiritual life commitment) has to take over in order to help a couple, who have individual wills and very different personalities, make it through the territory where the Incompatibility Monsters lie crouching and waiting. In this section, we will first cover some of the lighter issues where the Incompatibility Monsters find vulnerability and devour hapless travelers! Later, we will get into deeper areas.

Section 4   *Becoming One*

1. What are your hobbies? _____
   _____
   _____

2. What do you enjoy doing together? _____
   _____

3. What do you enjoy doing separately? _____
   _____

4. Are you energized by being alone—by having one-on-one, deeper friendships? Are you energized by being in groups of people, parties, gatherings, light friendships, etc.? Comment _____
   _____
   _____

5. Are there areas in your life that you devote huge amounts of time and attention to, such as career, hobbies, and pastimes? _____ If so, what are they? _____
   _____
   _____

6. What type recreation do you like? _____
   _____

7. How important is it for your mate to like the same interests, recreation, and entertainment?

   ☐ Very important   ☐ Moderately important   ☐ Not important at all

8. (Man)   Do you like to hang out with the guys? _____   How much? _____

9. (Woman)   Do you like to hang out with the gals? _____   How much? _____

10. (Man)   Are you comfortable with her associations? _____   The quantity of time? _____

11. (Woman)   Are you comfortable with his associations? _____   The quantity of time? _____

12. How important is it to have a good-looking spouse?

    ☐ Very Important   ☐ Moderately important   ☐ Not important at all

13. What is your idea of a good-looking man or woman? _____
    _____

Section 4   *Becoming One*

Section 4 **Becoming One**

14. On a scale of 1–5 (5 = a lot), how much does your fiancé(e)'s shape, physique, looks, voice, and mannerisms register on your attraction meter? _____

15. Is there anything about your fiancé(e)'s personality, character, behavior, or habits that you would like to be different or that displeases, annoys, or causes you concern? _____
    If so, what? _____
    _____
    _____

16. Is there anything about your looks, personality, character, etc. you would like to be different? _____
    If so, what? _____
    _____
    _____

17. How important is it to you to maintain a trim body and for your fiancé(e) to maintain a trim body?
    ☐ Very Important   ☐ Moderately important   ☐ Not important at all

18. Do you compare yourself or your fiancé(e) to others? _____ If so, how much?
    Comparing yourself   ☐ Never   ☐ Sometimes   ☐ Frequently   ☐ A lot – constantly
    Comparing your fiancé(e) ☐ Never   ☐ Sometimes   ☐ Frequently   ☐ A lot – constantly

19. Do you hope to change your spouse once you are married? _____ Or, do you think your spouse will naturally change in these areas by being married? _____

20. If your spouse never changes in these areas, can you live happily and contentedly with him/her for a half century or more without any possibility of, or hope for, those desired changes? _____

21. You may have answered these questions in the understandable state of infatuation. Eventually you might find that your attraction meter isn't registering as high as it does now. As stated elsewhere, you may not know yourself or your fiancé(e) well enough to see these things now, or you may be choosing to ignore or suppress things about your fiancé(e) that you wish were just a little different. Later into your marriage, you may find these feelings creeping to the surface. In that event, how will you deal with yourself and those feelings?
    _____
    _____
    _____
    _____
    _____

Section 4 — Becoming One

BOUNDARIES

One of the main themes of this book and of premarital preparation is the issue of two people bonding and becoming one flesh. Does the subject of boundaries have any place in such a book? After all, the thought of boundaries conjures up ideas about property lines, fences, and walls—things that are meant to divide, separate, keep people out, and distinguish one from another. In a book about coming together, dying to self, and drawing ever closer, what could possibly be the need for a discussion about boundaries? Well, becoming one flesh obviously does not mean that two people become one physical person. Although we marry and become *one flesh* in a lifelong covenant as the Bible states it, each is still an individual person.

Whatever else it may mean, becoming one flesh at least means becoming a partnership with a lifelong vision. How, then, do two individuals with unique wills and unique ideas and methods, unite and become one? The Bible says that if *any man is in Christ he is a new creature; old things have passed away and all things are new and all things are of God.* (See 2 Cor. 5:17.) Similarly, within marriage, the "you" is to die (so to speak) and become "us." As a single Christian, you are to live for God. Now, instead of living individually for God, you live *together* for God.

> Conflicts that are poorly handled create offenses, and offenses are nothing other than violations of another's soul, i.e., another's boundaries.

This is a nice theory, but what does it have to do with boundaries? In the process of becoming one, you will have to make adjustments (a.k.a. dying to self). Pressure, discomfort, and pain caused by conflicts, often accompany these adjustments. You likely have had disagreements or maybe even fights. If you haven't had any, you would do well to take a closer look at your internal world and see whether you are being honest about your feelings. Here is the point: conflicts that are poorly handled create offenses, and offenses are nothing other than violations of another's soul, another's boundaries.

Jesus instructs us to pray, "Forgive us our debts [trespasses, sins, offenses] as we forgive those who sin against us" (Matt. 6:12–15). He (incidentally) stated the case for individual boundaries. Offending or sinning against one another is tantamount to crossing another's boundary, and that is trespassing. It is also abuse. Within our marriages, we sometimes take each other for granted. This means we violate each other and don't even recognize we are doing it, or we harden our hearts and don't think the offense is such a big deal. Hence, we do not apologize, ask for forgiveness, and seek reconciliation. *This* is what builds walls of separation–not the fact of being unique, individual people with separate souls, hearts, minds, and wills.

Thus, there are two types of boundaries. One type differentiates us from one another but does not divide or separate us. The other type is a wall we put up to protect ourselves from harm, offense, and violation or to purposely squelch or destroy a relationship.

Section 4 — Becoming One

Forgiveness

 Matt. 6:12–15; 18:21–22   Mark 11:25–26   Luke 17:3–4   John 8:10–11

Forgiveness is a major theme of the Bible, and it has a lot to do with the subjects of bonding and boundaries. We are forgiven by God, and we are to forgive one another. However, some questions about forgiveness are often raised. Share your thoughts on the following.

1. Are you to forgive just because someone asks you to forgive him? (Luke 17:3–4) _____

2. Do there need be signs of repentance before you forgive? (Luke 17:3–4) _____

3. Is forgiveness conditional? (Matt. 6:12–15; Mark 11:25–26) _____

4. What happens if a person sins against you over and over—are you still to forgive? (Matt. 18:21–22)

5. Does forgiving someone excuse the behavior and set up him/her to sin again? (John 8:10–11)

6. If your fiancé(e) asks for forgiveness, do you forgive and let it go, or do you tuck it away and have a silent "let's see" or a "you must atone" attitude? _____

Section 4 — Becoming One

Self-esteem

READ | Matt. 16:24–25 | John 12:24-25 | Rom. 3:10, 23 | Rom. 7:24
Rom. 12:3 | 1 Cor. 1:29–31 | 1 Cor. 4:3–4 | 1 Pet. 1:18–19

Boundaries are not only about how you view and treat others. They are also about how you view and treat yourself and about how you let others treat you. Boundaries relate to our self-respect or lack of self-respect. Self-esteem is a similar and more popular term. Self-help books are full of talk about self-esteem and how to improve it. The concept is a major tenet of modern psychology. One problem with self-esteem is its immediate link to a preoccupation with self—the premier characteristic of this self-absorbed age. (2 Tim. 3:1–4) Conversely, the Bible speaks strongly about denying oneself and dying to self (Matt. 16:24–25; John 12:24–25). With such Scriptures in mind, is giving credence to self-esteem contradictory to biblical teaching? When we consider the actual meaning of the two words (the act of esteeming ourselves), the practice or pursuit of self-esteem is illogical, unbiblical, and unacceptable (1 Cor. 4:3–4; 2 Cor. 10:12). But, perhaps the term is valid in the sense that the way we view ourselves is also a statement about our view of God and our relationship to Him.

The concept of self-esteem is questionable. Our value to God is not (1 Pet. 1:18–19). However, we must keep in mind that such Scriptures serve to point our attention to God's love, grace, and mercy—not our lovability. It is very clear that while we were yet sinners, Christ loved us and died for us (Rom. 5:8–10). Therefore, self-esteem—our value and worth—is not intrinsic to us. There is no hint in the Bible of our natural worthiness (1 Cor. 1:29–31). Our worth is intrinsic to God, as evidenced by the value He places upon us and the cost He paid to redeem us.

Yet, it's not correct for Christians to wallow in self-abasement. God has redeemed us, washed us, and made us joint heirs with Jesus. Apostle Paul said he was the worst—the chief—of sinners, yet he didn't wallow in it.

It has been said that humility is the act of self-forgetfulness. Rather than being occupied with positive or negative thoughts about ourselves, we should be caught up in God—in His goodness, beauty, grace, and love. It has also been said that humility is the attitude of seeing ourselves as God sees us—no less and no more. A normal, healthy view of self is the biblical view of self.

1. Comment on what Matthew 16:24–25 means. _____

2. Comment on what 1 Peter 1:18–19 means. _____

3. What is the difference between biblical self-denial and such things as: self-deprecation, low self-esteem, inferiority, and worthlessness? (Rom. 7:24; 12:3; 1 Cor. 4:3–4)

_____
_____
_____
_____
_____

4. Comment about other things that support your self-worth (careers, skills, education, money, etc.)

_____
_____
_____
_____
_____

Your identity in Christ

5. In each category below, look up at least some of the verses on your identity in Christ.[3] Pick a few from each column and write a few sentences summarizing what each verse says about how God views you. Be prepared to read and discuss how these verses affect you and how you *own* them for yourself. Be sure to number each comment with the number preceding the Scripture reference or use the verse reference. Use additional paper if needed.

   Note: These verses are not listed to pump up a deflated ego, but rather to counter the very real attacks we constantly suffer from our enemy. Satan is called the accuser of the brethren (Rev. 12:10). From him comes the incessant barrage of thoughts that are accusative and meant to induce guilt, shame, hopelessness, discouragement, despair, and a sense of failure and defeat. (See John 8:44; 10:10.)

I am forgiven, redeemed, and reconciled		I am accepted		I am secure		I am significant
1. Isa. 53:1–12	10.	John 15:15	19.	John 1:12	28.	Matt. 5:13–14
2. Rom. 4:7	11.	Rom. 5:1	20.	Rom. 8:1	29.	John 1:12
3. Eph. 2:13	12.	1 Cor. 6:17	21.	Rom. 8:28–30	30.	John 15:5
4. Col. 1:14	13.	1 Cor. 6:20	22.	Rom. 8:33	31.	1 Cor. 3:16
5. Col. 2:13–14	14.	2 Cor. 5:21	23.	Rom. 8:35	32.	1 Cor. 12:27
6. 1 Pet. 3:18	15.	Eph. 1:5	24.	Phil. 1:6	33.	2 Cor. 5:17,18
7. Rom. 5:8	16.	Eph. 2:18–19	25.	Col. 1:13	34.	Eph. 1:1
8. Gal. 3:13	17.	Col. 1:14	26.	2 Tim. 1:7	35.	Eph. 2:6
9. Rev. 5:9	18.	Col. 2:10	27.	Heb. 4:16	36.	Eph. 2:10

---

[3] This list has been widely circulated. The original source of this compilation is unknown.

Ref # or verse ref	Summary

Section 4 — Becoming One

Ref # or verse ref	Summary

Section 4 — Becoming One

Your immune system at work

> *Casting down imaginations, and every high thing that exalts itself against the knowledge of God, and bringing into captivity every thought to the obedience of Christ.* (2 Cor. 10:5)

The immune system monitors and mobilizes the body against foreign and harmful invaders such as viruses, bacteria, and pollen. When the immune system is not working properly, it does not recognize these invaders as enemies. These foreign bodies sometimes masquerade as friends and piggyback onto healthy cells or tissue. Not only that, the immune system can be fooled into believing the body's own cells and tissues are "enemies" and begin attacking itself.

Our personhood also has an immune system. One aspect of our defense system is *boundaries*, and depending on the health of our immune system, we either reject harmful thoughts and emotions or we accept them and let them in–giving them a measure of control over us. The above Scripture is our spiritual, mental, and emotional immune system at work. A proper identity in Christ is our immune system at its core.

People who acquiesce to abuse have few boundaries and little sense of worth to protect them. Therefore, they let people use them and abuse them to one degree or another. Some even consider abuse (mild abuse, at least) a sign of attention and affection. For example, *someone cares enough about me to want to sleep with me*. Never mind that the other person doesn't want to be there in the morning–every morning–for the rest of his or her life. This is an example of one person feigning affection in order to exploit the other. And, it is an example of the other person not having healthy boundaries by his or her accepting the fakery and settling for mere imitation.

All of this talk about boundaries comes dramatically into play in resolving conflicts[4]—in standing up for principles, creating a loving home atmosphere, and setting godly standards for the way you treat each other and respond to each other. All of this can be summed up in two questions:

- How do you handle matters when you are the offender?
- How do you respond when you are the one offended?

To this end, we want you to develop the skill and habit of monitoring your thoughts, emotions, and responses. We want you to help each other evaluate your inner lives by being on the lookout for, and talking openly with each other about, such things as:

- Harmful (wrong) thinking
- Harmful (wrong) emotions
- Shame, guilt, fear
- Harmful, abusive behavior
- Harmful, abusive responses
- Abusive traits or habits

---

[4] Resolving conflicts is covered in the section on communication. The issue of boundaries is inherent in conflict resolution.

Section 4 — Becoming One

A SPORTS-HOBBY PRENUPTIAL

> *"Help, God! I married a football fanatic!"*
>
> *One newly married woman was greatly surprised to find out how much her husband liked watching football. He was so obsessed with it that for whole days on the weekends she felt completely ignored. Thanks to this sister's suggestion, we have devoted some space to the issue of compatibility in regards to marrying a sports maniac. I have since heard a new term for these women: sports widows.*

We are mindful of high-profile addictions such as drugs, alcohol, and porn, but let's give some attention to sports/hobby addictions, because these can be quite problematic in marriage. First, though, here is the basic thing you need to know about the difference between men and women:

Boys like to fall out of trees and break their arms, and girls like to hug dolls.

There! That's all you need to know about the man-woman relationship!

It is inconceivable to most women how men can enjoy smashing into each other at bone-crushing velocity and then get up, crack their helmets together, and give each other a pat on the behind. What sort of mixed message is this aggressive-passive behavior? *What species of animal is this,* she wonders? The issue is further complicated because a husband looks at his wife and says, "It's a guy thing; you wouldn't understand." And so, being a sensitive and thoughtful person, she comes to the only possible conclusion: *I married an idiot!*

Part of the marriage vows should include an agreement on the amount of time a man (or woman) can devote to sports and hobbies–whether dirt biking, tennis, fishing and hunting, golfing, and, of course, football. So, let's get to the issue at hand: **A Sports-Hobby Prenuptial Survey**

1. Are you, or is your fiancé(e), obsessed with sports or hobbies? You ____   Your fiancé(e) ____

2. On a scale of 1 to 5, how much do you like sports/hobbies of any kind? You ____ Your fiancé(e)___

3. How many hours per week or weekend do you devote to recreation, sports/hobbies? _____

4. How many hours per week or weekend will you be comfortable with your spouse watching or playing sports or doing his/her hobbies? _____

5. How much will you want or expect your spouse to be interested in the sports, etc., that interest you?
   ☐ Not at all   ☐ A little interested   ☐ Moderately interested   ☐ A lot of interest

6. How much will you actually be interested in your spouse's sports or hobbies?
   ☐ Not at all   ☐ A little interested   ☐ Moderately interested   ☐ A lot of interest

7. How much will you expect your spouse to be interested in you during sports weekends, which nowadays, is every weekend?
   ☐ Not at all   ☐ A little interested   ☐ Moderately interested   ☐ A lot of interest

Section 4   ***Becoming One***

8. On a scale of 1–5 (5 meaning you watch sports a lot) Rate yourself and your fiancé(e) on watching televised sports. You _____ Your fiancé(e) _____

9. How much do you actively (actually) participate in sports and recreational activities?

   ☐ Not at all   ☐ A little   ☐ Moderately   ☐ A lot

10. What kind of sports/recreation do you like? _____
    _____
    _____

11. Are there other activities your fiancé(e) participates in for which you have no interest? _____
    Which ones? _____
    _____
    _____

Television and Movies

12. How much time per week or weekend do you spend watching TV or movies? _____

13. Do you watch daytime TV? _____ If so, what programs? _____
    _____

14. What other kind of programs do you watch? _____
    _____

15. Do you like romantic movies (chick flicks)? _____ Does your fiancé(e)? _____

16. Do you like action movies (guy flicks)? _____ Does your fiancé(e)? _____

17. Do you want or expect your fiancé(e) to watch your kind of programs with you? _____

18. Will it hurt your feelings if he/she doesn't cuddle with you and watch your programs? _____

Circle the number that reflects your level of agreement.   Disagree ⇐   Agree ⇒

19. I enjoy watching movies and TV programs.   1   2   3   4   5

20. I do not watch TV, movies, or videos. They are a waste of time.   1   2   3   4   5

21. Most TV programs and movies are unwholesome, ungodly, and sinful.   1   2   3   4   5

Section 4 — Becoming One

WORKAHOLISM

As with sports and hobbies, work can be a source of trouble. Not only are some people obsessed with sports and recreation, but also some are obsessed with work. This too, is a common problem and very fertile ground for neglect, abuse, discontent, and conflict. Some people are so driven in their occupation or career (and let's not forget ministry) that they neglect other important areas of their life; namely, their family.

Balancing family time with a career, business, or job is not an easy task. It is easier if you have an eight-hour job that you don't take home with you. But if you are building a business or climbing the corporate ladder, you will experience conflict of interest and conflict of time.

A workaholic, like an alcoholic or other addictive personality, is a person whose life is out of balance. There are at least two motivating factors for a workaholic. They are:

- Ambition (noble and ignoble): a desire to get ahead and be the provider, the desire for wealth, greed, a competitive nature, the need to win, to be on top, and to achieve (including the drive to achieve in ministry).

- Avoidance: A drive emanating from a need to avoid uncomfortable issues and situations. Workaholism might be a way to avoid facing the truth about oneself. Ironically, it might be a way of covering up and compensating for insecurities. Likewise, it might be a way of avoiding uncomfortable or painful relationship issues such as emotional and spiritual closeness—issues that require vulnerability, transformation, repentance, dying to self, bonding, and becoming one.

So, if either of you is a *driven* personality—working long hours as a matter of choice when there is no financial crunch—you would do well at this point to slow down and take an honest look at your situation.

Your fiancé(e)'s ambitious nature might impress you now as being a desire to get ahead and provide a better life for both of you. Later into your marriage, however, those same traits might be the things you come to hate because they take supremacy over your personal relationship and the welfare of your children. A person's occupation or ministry can consume them, so you would be wise to consider this. Again, this is a personality, temperament, or character trait, and it can be dormant and unseen—waiting for the right circumstances and conditions before it manifests.

1. a. On a scale of 1–5, how ambitious are you, how driven or given to your work or ministry? _____

   b. On a scale of 1–5, how ambitious is your fiancé(e), how driven or given to work or ministry? _____

2. What are your occupational goals? _____

3. Using one word (or a few), describe your attitude about work. _____

4. Finish the sentence: Work is _____

5. What do you like about your work? _____

6. What do you not like about your work? _____
_____
_____

7. Some occupations require enormous amounts of time and commitment. If such is your situation, are you prepared for the sacrifice it will take in other areas of your life, such as your marriage relationship and your children? Comment _____
_____
_____

8. Are you willing to sacrifice your marriage and your children for your or your spouse's career? ____

9. Are you willing to forgo having children if you have a consuming occupation or lifestyle? ____

10. Is either of you attending college, finishing your education or occupational training? ____

11. Is yours a "put-hubby-through-school" situation? ____

12. Why do you suppose putting a husband through school could damage the relationship?
_____
_____
_____

13. If money, education, or other considerations were not an issue, so that you could do anything you wanted to do and the means and opportunity were provided, what would you want to do?
_____
_____

14. In the same way, if your fiancé(e) could do anything he or she wanted to do, what would that be?
_____
_____

15. Do you have a vision for ministry or a particular calling, vocation, or lifestyle? ____
    If so, what is it? _____
_____
_____

16. Does your fiancé(e) share the same vision? _____
_____
_____

Section 4 — Becoming One

Summing it up

Questions 13–16 are not for wishful thinking. Their purpose is to explore your true interest and passion. This is important as you seek direction for your lives. Perhaps you have a strong desire to be a missionary, to work in a rescue mission, or to be in some other such service. If that is the case, you need to make that a nonnegotiable part of your life and find someone who shares the same passion and vision. Compatibility in your vision for your marriage and family is crucial.

Marriage radically changes your life. Things will never be as they were when you were single. While single, you can do as you please. You can be self-centered. But, once you marry, all of that changes—your life is no longer your own. Your very life becomes a partnership. Some people do not realize the drastic changes that must occur to achieve the one-flesh union. They think things can continue pretty much as they were when single. It's just not so.

> **In marriage, neither one has "rights" apart from the well-being, needs, and desires of the other.**

Returning to the sports example, although you can substitute career or other things, some guys are avid sportsman. While single, they spend a lot of time pursuing those things, and they have a right to do so. Since this is their lifestyle while single, they might expect to continue with it when married. If that is the case, they need a reality check. Either that or they had better find a wife who is honestly content to have her husband consumed with those things. Why? Because it will greatly affect the amount of attention left for her and the family. **Speaking to the woman, if you are not up for this, or if it will put your children at risk of neglect, do not marry him.** If you *do* marry him anyway, you mustn't start complaining later into your marriage that he doesn't spend enough time with you and the kids, that he's obsessed with other things, or that he wants to hang a moose head on your living room wall! The situation was there before you married, but you did not want to face it, or else you thought it would change when married or you thought you could change him.

Likewise, single women have the right to pursue their calling, passion, and lifestyle. If a single woman wants to marry and desires to be an at-home mom and have six children, she has a right to that. Her temptation might be to settle for a man who is adamant about wanting only two kids (or none). If, instead, she enjoys a career, she might expect to continue as a career woman after marriage. If that is the case, she needs to find a man who supports her desires without feelings of competition, neglect, or insecurity. Again, think of your future kids.

The point is this: If your mate has strong interests while single, do not expect he or she will (or even should) give them up after marriage unless it's agreed upon before marriage and it's a joyful, willing choice beforehand to do so. Another way of saying this is you must not pull a *bait and switch* maneuver on one another.[5] This, of course, does not take into account situations beyond your control such as accidents, sickness, downsizing, or quintuplets! These events will and should legitimately and naturally change things and cause you to rearrange your lives. **But, beyond all the possible scenarios, the bottom line is this: in marriage, neither person has so-called rights apart from the well-being, needs, and desires of the other.**

In short, what we are saying is that some people want to be married so much and for emotionally immature reasons that they are willing to compromise themselves—thinking perhaps his or her spouse will "mellow out" or can be changed once married. And that truly *is* wishful thinking.

---

[5] Sometimes, in the state of infatuation and while dating, one person shows enjoyment in the other's interests. The woman, for example, shares his interest in car races; the man shares her interest for concerts. Neither one, however, actually enjoys the other's interests. When married, they let the artificial interest evaporate.

Section 4 — Becoming One

SKELETONS IN THE CLOSET

Have you shared every element of your life, past and present, which might be a factor in your marriage union? Is there anything in your closet that you would rather not share? Is there something you have held back from your fiancé(e) out of fear of rejection or shame? Do you subscribe to the adage that says, "What he/she doesn't know won't hurt him/her"?

If this is you, to any degree, you must now come out of the closet. There is (or used to be), a point in marriage ceremonies where the officiate said something like *"If there is anyone who has a just reason why this couple should not be married, let him speak now or forever hold his peace."* That is what we are after here. Is there anything in your past or present that, if your fiancé(e) knew, would be–or might possibly be–a "deal breaker"? **If so, now is the time!**

To what degree you share, and your motive for sharing, should be considered. The principle to adhere to is love—the honest desire to protect your mate rather than your secrets and your image. Share what is necessary to establish a truthful, honest, and faithful union. For example, your fiancé(e) does not need to hear the explicit sexual details of any former relationships. If your fiancé(e) wants or demands to hear the explicit details of a former intimacy, it might be a sign of insecurity, jealousy, bitterness, or subdued anger and rage that will show up in the future. If that is the case, you will want to take a closer look at your fiancé(e)'s request to know the details and whether he or she has unresolved issues that would be detrimental to your union.

Some things you do want to establish: Is there a shameful or traumatic incident(s) that you have not revealed? Do you have unrevealed debt? Were either of you arrested, charged, or imprisoned and are withholding that information? Are you now, or were you ever involved in pornography, homosexuality/lesbianism, drug abuse, child molesting, prostitution, physical abuse, or any other criminal, sinful, or aberrant behavior? If you do not reveal such things, they could surface later and cause distrust and trouble. In order to have true companionship, you need to know that your spouse loves you and accepts you fully—no matter what you did in your past.

> We live in an extremely self-centered and mobile society. When it comes to dating and seeking a faithful life partner, this self-centeredness and mobility fosters a lack of accountability and a lack of history. This lack, for example, is a prominent feature of Internet dating, and it often leads to dead-end relationships or worse—manifold troubles and regrets.
>
> With society the way it is, we are not hesitant to suggest a professional background check **before getting emotionally involved** or considering someone as a mate. You might scoff at this idea, but it has merit. Even without a *professional* background check, you should personally check with your prospective spouse's relatives, friends, and even a former spouse and former in-laws. A former spouse may be bitter and may have been the cause of the trouble. His or her attitude might skew the response. Then again, he or she might have some illuminating facts that would help you see things more clearly. This is especially true in the case of an abuser—a person who is wonderful in public but who is a different person privately.

1. Would you consider it a lack of trust if you did background and credit checks on each other? _____

2. In light of the above, and to finish this section on becoming one, answer this one last question. *Are you being completely honest with yourself and your mate about who you are and what you have done?* (Yes/No) _____

 Now, in the presence of God and your mentors, pastor, or counselor, take turns looking each other in the eye and ask this exact question of each other. "Are you being completely honest with me about who you are and about your past—what you have done and what you have experienced?"

NOTES

Section 5   *Extended Relationships*

EXTENDED RELATIONSHIPS

YOUR FAMILY AND FUTURE IN-LAWS

Parents and in-laws can either bless or curse a union. Tough words, huh? Most of the time, a couple's relationship to parents and in-laws is a blessing and complementary to their union. Usually, by the time children reach adulthood, parents are quite ready to let go of the reins. Sometimes, that is not the case. Then, again, to be fair to parents, marriage isn't just about you and you. It's about you and you, and a host of relatives—all of whom will be bound up with you to one degree or another in your union.

Ideally, your parents will bond with your spouse, and he or she will become their new son or daughter. That's how close it becomes. Additionally, you will most likely make grandparents of your parents. That further welds the bond and strengthens it with steel girders and steel cables. Put simply, your decision will affect many people, and they, as well as you, will either be blessed or cursed by your union and by your decisions and behavior within your union.

1. What do your parents, other family members, and friends think of your fiancé(e) and your pending union? _____

2. Describe the relationship between you and your future in-laws. _____

3. Do your parents and future in-laws relate to each other? If not, why? Describe their relationship.

4. Do your parents or in-laws meddle in your lives? _____ If yes, how do you respond to them, and how does your fiancé(e) respond to them? _____

5. List any conflicts with your parents or future in-laws. _____

Section 5   **Extended Relationships**

FAMILY AND IN-LAW CHECKLIST

Rate yourself and then your mate on the following statements about parents and in-law relationships.

0 = not at all   **1** = somewhat or occasionally   **2** = moderately   **3** = often or very much

Rate yourselves   You   Fiancé(e)

1. Dependent upon parents for emotional/decision-making help. ... _____ _____
2. Allow parent(s) to be too involved in your relationship. .... _____ _____
3. Dependent upon parent's financial help. .... _____ _____
4. Critical about your fiancé(e) to your parent(s). .... _____ _____
5. Seek parents' advice about your relationship. .... _____ _____
6. Desire to please parents. .... _____ _____
7. Have well-balanced relationship with both sets of parents. .... _____ _____
8. Gossip to parents about your fiancé(e) .... _____ _____
9. Put your parents needs/wants above your fiancé(e) .... _____ _____
10. Thoughtfully consider your parent's opinions of your fiancé(e) . _____ _____

Rate your parents   Your parents   Fiancé(e) parents

11. They interfere or are overly involved in our relationship. .... _____ _____
12. They are indifferent to our relationship – not interested. .... _____ _____
13. They are overly involved in wedding planning. .... _____ _____
14. They are uninvolved in wedding planning. .... _____ _____
15. They are supportive of our union. .... _____ _____
16. They have a good relationship with my fiancé(e)'s parents. .... _____ _____
17. They are jealous of our relationship. .... _____ _____
18. They feel rejected because of our relationship. .... _____ _____

Any other comments? _____

_____

Section 5   Extended Relationships

PREVIOUS RELATIONSHIPS [1]

Live-in relationships and long-term intimate relationships are prevalent in our society. One consequence of this unfortunate trend is that the word "spouse" is frequently replaced with words such as "partner," "mate," or "significant other." Rather than repeating tedious relationship options, I have opted to use the term "former mate" to refer to an ex-spouse or any intimate (emotionally or sexually bonded) relationships you have had.

1. How many times have you been married or had intimate or significant relationships? _____

2. What was the cause of each relationship ending? _____

3. What did your former mate do to end it? _____

4. What was your part in the failure? _____

5. What was your former mate(s) like? _____

6. Was a former mate abusive in anyway? _____ Explain _____

7. What is your relationship like now with your former mate(s)? _____

8. Do you compare your fiancé(e) (either favorably or unfavorably) to a former relationship? _____

---

[1] This part is about issues relating to divorce or the end of "significant relationships" ***by choice***. The situation of widows and widowers is not specifically addressed. Although a different approach is needed for people in this category, what follows will be useful for them.

Section 5   **Extended Relationships**

9. Is your fiancé(e) a springboard away from the negativity of a former relationship? _____

10. Are you on the rebound? _____ Does your relationship have elements of a rebound? _____

11. If children necessitate it, how would you characterize contact with your former mate(s)?

    ☐ Amicable   ☐ Combative   ☐ Dangerous/volatile   ☐ Nonexistent

Name of your children	Age	Name of other parent	How involved is he/she in child's life? Characterize their relationship.

12. Do you speak respectfully and graciously of your former mate? _____

13. Does your fiancé(e) speak respectfully and graciously of his/her former mate? _____

14. Will you check with each other's former mate and his/her family and friends to verify the facts of the old relationship? _____ If not, why not? _____
_____
_____

15. Would it be an act of mistrust if either of you checked with your fiancé(e)'s former mate, former in-laws and family, and former friends? _____ Comment _____
_____
_____

16. Is it possible that your fiancé(e)'s former mate and family will have some relevant and illuminating information—perhaps a different story? _____ Comment _____
_____
_____

17. Are you paying or receiving alimony, child support? _____

18. Has someone ever put a restraining order or a do-not-contact order on you? _____ Have you put one on anybody? _____ Comment _____
_____

19. Do you foresee any trouble from your or your fiancé(e)'s former mate? _____ Comment _____
_____
_____

Section 5 — Extended Relationships

20. a. Have you met or had phone contact with your fiancé(e)'s former mate? _____ Describe the contact.
    _____
    _____

    b. If no contact, why not? _____
    _____
    _____

21. What do you think of your fiancé(e)'s former mate? _____
    _____
    _____

22. a. Toward your fiancé(e)'s former mate: Do you feel love, compassion, and understanding? Do you feel anger, jealousy, resentment, rage, or threatened? _____
    _____
    _____
    _____

    b. When you see your fiancé(e)'s former mate, what do you feel? What is your emotional response?
    _____
    _____
    _____

23. Does your fiancé(e) have too much contact with his or her former mate? _____
    _____
    _____

24. Is your fiancé(e) still emotionally tied to or too chummy with his/her former mate? _____
    _____
    _____

25. Aside from this course, what other steps have you taken to prepare for combining your lives? What other materials, resources, classes, counseling, etc. have you implemented and completed?
    _____
    _____

Section 5 — Extended Relationships

DIVORCED AND REMARRYING

Within the body of Christ, there are differing views about divorce and remarriage. Some denominations (pastor, teachers, counselors, authors, etc.) adhere strictly to Matthew 19:9 in which Jesus says adultery is the only permissible reason for divorce. From that position, there are varying views and doctrines all the way to the opposite pole which accepts divorce and remarriage almost without question. The attitude of the first camp might be characterized as, *Jesus was explicit, and that settles it*. For the other camp, it is not so cut and dry. For them, the question is whether other extenuating circumstances exist that make divorce an option— situations that Jesus would not have intended to exclude in his reply to the Pharisees—situations, for example, that make marriage a cruel and life-threatening bondage.

This polarization seemingly reduces the first camp to a rigid, legalist group devoid of compassion while reducing the second camp to a carnal, Bible-distorting group desperately bent on finding loopholes for their willful disobedience. We gracefully suggest that neither is generally the case for these groups.

Many churches address the needs of divorced, single parent, and stepfamily situations. At the same time, however, divorce must be addressed at its root: namely, disobedience to God. It is the duty of pastors and the church body to *enforce* [2] the sobering commands and responsibility of obedience to God upon engaged and married couples.

Furthermore, most people want to get married in church i.e., before God and witnesses and by God's officially ordained minister. But they don't go to God and the church to get divorced. That comment might sound crass. Nevertheless, it does seem we want our marriages to be sanctioned and blessed by God, but any man-made court and judge will suffice for divorce. We do not look to the church to approve or to bless our divorce—especially when we lack biblical grounds.

One popular speaker and writer has precisely stated, "We don't have a marriage crisis in the Christian community; we have a crisis of faith."[3] Put in other words, many who profess Christ do not obey Him (Matt. 7:21). The admonition in James 2:20, "faith without works is dead," might more readily be grasped if said this way, "Faith without **obedience** is dead."

Whether you had biblical grounds for divorce and whether you have biblical grounds for remarriage *is* a question that needs to be answered. Above this is the ultimate question of whether you, as a professing Christian, love God and are living for Him by honoring and obeying Him with your whole mind, your whole will, and your whole life, including your decision to remarry (Matt. 22:36–37; Jn. 14:15). Are you obeying God and His Word? Are you putting the sacredness of marriage above your own feelings and desires, or are you putting your feelings, pleasures, comfort, desires, and perceived needs above the Word of God and the sacredness of marriage?

Although at this point you are likely far along in your relationship and committed to remarrying, we nevertheless encourage you to seek competent, dedicated resources on divorce and remarriage. On the next page, we will present a few questions. Knowing we cannot cover all the bases in this section, we simply refer you to the following two resources, which carefully and systematically cover the topics of divorce and remarriage. We hope that your church or your mentors have these or other excellent resources available for you to use.

Suggested assignment

Jay Adams, *Marriage, Divorce, and Remarriage in the Bible* (Zondervan)

Pastor Alistair Begg, *We Two Are One* audio series.
> Included in this series is a sermon on divorce and remarriage, which can be ordered separately. With compassion and yet sobering clarity, Alistair presents the mandate to honor and obey God in your marriage covenant as well as in your decision to remarry. Available at http://www.truthforlife.org

---

[2] Church discipline is a forgotten aspect and practice of body life. Perhaps it will be restored in the Church. (See Matt. 18:15–20; 1 Cor. 5:1–13)

[3] Emerson Eggerichs, *Love and Respect* A Focus On The Family Book (Nashville: Thomas Nelson, Inc. 2004), 276.

Section 5 — Extended Relationships

The following questions are not intended to be judgmental, legalistic, or dictatorial. They *are* meant to hold up Scripture as the authority and standard for your decisions and motives. Many Christians divorce without biblical grounds. Furthermore, it is often the case that extreme circumstances such as abuse are not the issue. Christians use the same reasons the world uses: incompatibility or irreconcilable differences. This survey isn't a faultfinding mission, but rather a mission to help you order your lives according to the Bible and, as Jesus commanded, to die to self—to self-centered feelings, thoughts, choices, and behavior.

1. Is your divorce final? _____ What date was it finalized? _____

2. If your divorce is not final, on what biblical authority do you involve yourself in this relationship?
   _____
   _____

3. Who instigated the divorce? _____

4. What were the biblical grounds for your divorce? Include Scripture verses. _____
   _____
   _____
   _____

5. Other than biblical grounds, what was the reason for your divorce? _____
   _____
   _____
   _____

6. What are the biblical grounds for your remarriage? Include Scripture verses. _____
   _____
   _____
   _____

7. If your former mate has not remarried, does he or she want to reconcile? _____ (1 Cor. 7:10–15)
   If your former mate wants to reconcile and remarry, what are your biblical grounds for not doing so?
   _____
   _____

8. Any further comments about divorce and remarriage? _____
   _____
   _____

Section 5 — Extended Relationships

STEPFAMILIES

The issue of two people bonding and becoming one flesh is one thing. The issue of joining two families into one family is an altogether different matter, and it deserves a huge amount of consideration–something that we can only touch on here.[4] If you are considering entering, or have already committed to a stepfamily marriage, we strongly encourage you to read some books on stepfamilies–notably *The Smart Stepfamily* by Ron Deal, Bethany House Publishers. It is a fair-minded, balanced dose of reality. **We strongly suggest that you read this book**.

> **Suggested assignment**
>
> *The Smart Stepfamily*
>
> by Ron Deal

Along with reading this book, we urge you to invest a lot of time to learn about stepfamilies. You can do this by finding a counselor who specializes in this area, by finding a stepfamily ministry or group, and by doing your own research. There are many Web sites as well as books, seminars, CDs and videos where you can get quality information and help.

Why are we so adamant about going slower and doing a lot of homework? The stepfamily couples we have taken through premarital preparation have had little idea of what they were doing and what they were about to experience. Usually their ideas and expectations are vastly different from the realities of step parenting and stepfamily dynamics. To be fair, some couples and stepfamilies have a relatively easy time of it. However, some of the stories we have heard have been horrible. In addition, some stepfamily couples we have worked with have never read a book or listened to a recording on the subject. They blithely imagine that children, ex-spouses, and ex-in-laws will embrace the new situation and that everyone will cooperate. Sometimes it works, but when it doesn't, it can be hell on earth. Second (third, etc.) marriages can easily be torn apart by children, ex-spouses, and ex-in-laws. There can be visitation and custodial wars, conflict over discipline and parenting styles, jealousy, favoritism, bitterness, suspicion, anger, sabotage, betrayals, lying, slander, accusations, and many other emotional and relational sorrows and wounds. If biologically intact marriages can become a battlefield (which is rampant), stepfamily marriages can become more so, and they often do.

Lovely, huh? There's nothing like a cheery, positive, faith-filled bit of encouragement!

Perhaps you are wondering who would ever marry into a situation like this. Or perhaps you're wondering who the dour person who writes this stuff is? Actually, we have a lot of laughter in our premarital meetings, and mostly they are a lot of fun. But, we are also practical; we have had our wake-up moments with couples in crisis. Our motto, therefore, is "Hope for the best; prepare for the worst." That's a good motto, isn't it?

The following survey covers some significant issues regarding stepfamily unions. There are many resources on the Internet. Just type in stepfamily, stepfamily issues, step parenting, or some other such words in your search engine and you will have more information than you can handle. Again, however, Ron Deal's book, in our opinion, is the essential starting point.[5]

All of this is within the topic of bonding. The previous section was about the bonding between you and your spouse. This part, assuming it applies to you, is about the bonding that will or will not happen between you, your spouse, and all the stepchildren and extended stepfamily relatives.

---

[4] Uniting two families deserves a complete course of its own with dedicated books and other resources presented by those experienced in this area. We hope that your church or mentors require and provide this further, specific preparation.

[5] Ron Deal's Web site is http://www.smartstepfamilies.com. Another site is National Stepfamily Resource Center at http://www.stepfamilies.info/.

Section 5 — Extended Relationships

STEPFAMILY BELIEF SURVEY

Circle your level of agreement on the following:

Disagree ← | Agree →

	Totally Disagree	Mildly Disagree	Maybe 50/50	Mildly Agree	Totally Agree
1. We will not have much of a problem with blending our families.	1	2	3	4	5
2. Because we love each other, all of our children will love our union.	1	2	3	4	5
3. I expect my stepchildren to call me Mom (or Dad).	1	2	3	4	5
4. I want my stepchildren to be comfortable calling me Mom (or Dad.)	1	2	3	4	5
5. I want my spouse to discipline my children as he or she sees fit.	1	2	3	4	5
6. Children can feel betrayed by a new marriage.	1	2	3	4	5
7. Our children will easily adjust to the new living situation.	1	2	3	4	5
8. It will take about 6–12 months for our families to become a team.*	1	2	3	4	5
9. My children blame my ex-spouse or me for breaking up the home.	1	2	3	4	5
10. My children blame themselves for the divorce.	1	2	3	4	5
11. My children have anger or other emotional problems.	1	2	3	4	5
12. My children are very happy that I am remarrying.	1	2	3	4	5
13. My children are on mood-altering medications.	1	2	3	4	5
14. Our sexual union might trouble our children.	1	2	3	4	5
15. My ex-spouse will cause as much trouble as he or she can.	1	2	3	4	5
16. Some children experience great turmoil over the sexual union of their parent and stepparent.	1	2	3	4	5
17. My ex-spouse will be helpful and understanding and will work to support my new relationship.	1	2	3	4	5
18. Children should be protected as much as possible from knowing the nitty-gritty sins of their parents.	1	2	3	4	5
19. My fiancé(e)'s children have a lot of fun with me and will continue to do so after the wedding.	1	2	3	4	5
20. My fiancé(e)'s ex-spouse is so abusive to his/her children that they will naturally warm up to me (and likely prefer me to the abusive parent).	1	2	3	4	5
21. I will not interfere with the biological parent's method of discipline or lack of discipline.	1	2	3	4	5
22. Stepchildren never conspire to make life miserable for the new husband and wife.	1	2	3	4	5
23. My primary responsibility before my own desires is the protection and well-being of my children.	1	2	3	4	5
24. If my fiancé(e)'s children or my children are against this marriage, we should not go through with it.	1	2	3	4	5
25. In the decision to remarry, the emotional, physical, and spiritual well-being of my children and my fiancé(e)'s children is, by far, the most important consideration before my own needs and desires.	1	2	3	4	5

Section 5 — Extended Relationships

Summing up extended relationships

Anytime there is a marriage and then a divorce, shattered and fragmented hearts and souls result. After all, when two become one and then that bond is severed, what does that leave each person with? Their identity as a union–as one flesh–has been annihilated. The family unit–the family identity–has been annihilated. Now there are two fragmented people and likely also fragmented children, grandparents, and extended families. Every time a person marries and then divorces, a little bit more of that person's soul is fragmented or locked up, thus making it unavailable in future relationships—like a hard drive with unusable space.[6] Do you understand that those marrying for the second or third time might still have emotional ties to former spouses or that they might hold something of themselves back and have an issue with trust? How do couples bond when (metaphorically speaking) each has only a half, a third, or a quarter of a heart left? Bonding and giving your whole heart or what is left of it, for the second, third, or forth time presents many challenges. The forces against such bonding occurring are mighty and many.

Do you know that you know this person?

Trust is one of the big issues for couples who divorce and remarry—more so than for first time marriages, because in a first marriage, trust hasn't yet been broken. The idea of doing background checks, whether criminal, financial, or with former family members may seem to be a sign of distrust. It may seem to be building your relationship on distrust and suspicion from the very beginning, and after all, your relationship must be one of trust and faith. In our experience, there has been at least one instance where such a check would have revealed necessary facts that had been covered up. The marriage lasted for six harsh months. You do not want to go through your life being suspicious, and we do not want to foster suspicion. We are only seeking to foster accountability and full disclosure—something human nature often likes to avoid. For some couples, a background check would be advisable, but for others, it would never even be an issue.

* Following up on question 8, sources state that it takes **5 to 7 years** for stepfamilies to adapt and for their stress levels to match those of couples married for the first time.[7]

---

[6] A figure of speech, but you get the point. Former unions now torn apart create complex issues and life situations—things God never intended.

[7] Ron L. Deal, *The Smart Stepfamily* (Minneapolis: Bethany House Publishers, 2002) 25. Citing E.M. Hetherington and J. Kelly, *For Better or For Worse: Divorce Reconsidered* (New York: W.W. Norton & Company, 2002)

ROLES & EXPECTATIONS

Everyone entering marriage does so with ideas about what his or her relationship and lifestyle will be like. Because of family modeling and other life lessons, each person enters marriage with his or her own perspectives. Each person has unspoken rules of behavior that they assume are the universally correct and accepted behaviors and values. In short, the way we see things is the way we think they are and the way they should be seen.

During dating and engagement, we sometimes get a general, and often a vague, idea about our fiancé(e). Sometimes the person we see is the person *we want to see*. Some people build up those ideals to a high degree of expectation, and it's with those expectations in mind that they commit to marriage. When the ideal does not manifest, it jeopardizes the foundation of the relationship.

In the excitement of falling in love, we think we are tailor made for each other like a pair of fine-fitting gloves. The problem is, until you marry and live together, you haven't actually put the gloves on. Do not construe this as an excuse or an endorsement for test-driving your relationship by having sex and/or living together. Doing so is nothing other than basing your relationship on performance, and a performance-based relationship is definitely not what you want. A trial relationship is a pseudo commitment. It looks sort of like the real deal, but it isn't. **It undermines the foundation and opportunity for unconditional commitment**.[1]

Well, if people don't live together first, how will they know if they are compatible? Commitment must have a reasonable, effective test, and compatibility and expectations are part of the equation. The premarital preparation you are doing includes such things as your individual communion with God, counseling, personal inventories, books, classes, seminars, and input from family and friends. Additionally, it should include a long enough history with each other to ascertain habits, personalities, character and ethics, conflict resolution skills, and responses to stress and crisis. These are trustworthy means of determining compatibility and readiness for marriage. And this is what you are doing. All the effort you are putting forth cannot guarantee your relationship (you still have to walk the talk), but it puts you at a better starting place than those who do not put forth effort to prepare, to learn, and to change.

Roles, expectations, and goals are important topics to discuss. If, for example, you enjoy attending plays, operas, or political events, or if you enjoy spending your weekends restoring classic cars or watching sports, you likely have an unspoken assumption and expectation of continuing to do so. This section gives you the opportunity to discuss your expectations and hopes regarding your relationship, family, lifestyle, career choices, etc.

---

[1] See Myths About Cohabitation in the appendix.

Section 6   ***Roles and Expectations***

RELATIONSHIP EXPECTATIONS

1. Amos 3:3 encapsulates a theme consistent throughout this course and, pointedly, throughout this section on roles, expectations, and hopes. Comment about how the verse applies to your union.

   _____
   _____
   _____
   _____

2. Does your family's way of relating resemble the way your fiancé(e)'s family relates? _____

   _____
   _____

3. List some of your similar family lifestyles, views, relationship methods, etc.

   _____
   _____
   _____
   _____

4. List some of your different family lifestyles, views, relationship methods, etc.

   _____
   _____
   _____
   _____

5. What hopes or expectations do your have of your spouse? Finish the following sentence: I expect my spouse to _____

   _____
   _____
   _____

6. Are your hopes and expectations based on your upbringing? _____ If not, where did you get these views, desires, and expectations? _____

   _____
   _____

Section 6 — Roles and Expectations

7. How is your fiancé(e) in agreement with your expectations? _____

8. Does your fiancé(e) have any expectations or hopes of you (either realistic or unrealistic)? _____
   If so, what are they? _____

9. When married, how will you respond if your spouse does not agree with or meet your expectations?

10. Do you have additional comments you wish to make about hopes or expectations?

Section 6 — Roles and Expectations

ROLES & RESPONSIBILITY

Unspoken rules and roles

Each of us enters marriage with a host of preconceived ideas about rules and roles. We get these ideas from childhood upbringing—our family's way of doing things—and from peers, school, society, our own personalities, and the way we choose to respond to life. We call these things unspoken rules and roles because we generally take them for granted, and we mistakenly assume that our spouse does also. We assume that he or she sees things the way we see them. When we find out otherwise, it can be a shock, and it can cause great conflict. This is part of the drama of starting and establishing a brand new and unique family.

It behooves both of you to explore and talk about what might be your hidden, unspoken, or assumed rules and roles. You can save yourselves confusion, misunderstanding, and a lot of grief and conflict if you do this. There are many such unspoken, *assumed* rules and roles. We can't list or presume to know all of them, but here are a few to get you started in that direction.

- Don't reveal family secrets
- Help a woman to be seated at a dining table
- Discuss (or don't discuss) certain subjects
- Wash dishes immediately after each meal
- Public display of intimacy (holding hands, kissing)
- Don't let anyone know you're having problems
- Always (or never) open doors for woman
- Decision making is the husband's role
- Say grace (or not) before each meal
- Dress codes: hair, neckline, jewelry, cosmetics

1. Using a few descriptive words, list some of the unspoken rules or roles from your upbringing.
   _____
   _____
   _____

2. Check the roles/responsibilities you see for your fiancé(e) and yourself. Y = You F = Fiancé(e)

Y	F		Y	F		Y	F	
☐	☐	Provider	☐	☐	Cook	☐	☐	Kids' coach
☐	☐	Homemaker	☐	☐	Nurse/family health	☐	☐	Peacemaker
☐	☐	House cleaner	☐	☐	Laundry/seamstress	☐	☐	Bookkeeper
☐	☐	Driver/chauffeur	☐	☐	Social planner	☐	☐	Soccer mom/dad
☐	☐	Handyman	☐	☐	Activities director	☐	☐	Money manager
☐	☐	Spiritual leader	☐	☐	Child disciplinarian	☐	☐	_____
☐	☐	Gardener	☐	☐	Child educator	☐	☐	_____

3. Who is going to be the major breadwinner? _____

4. Who will be the major decision maker? _____

5. **(Man)** I want my wife to: ☐ Stay at home   ☐ Work outside home   ☐ Doesn't matter

6. **(Woman)** I want to: ☐ Stay at home   ☐ Work outside home   ☐ Doesn't matter

Section 6 — Roles and Expectations

Husband's role   (To be answered by both)

| 1 Cor. 11:3 | 2 Cor. 10:1 | Gal. 5:22–23 | Eph. 5:21–33 |
| 1Thes. 2:7–8 | 1 Tim. 3:1–12 | 2 Tim. 2:24–25 | Jas. 3:17–18 |

7. The Bible states that the husband is the head of the wife (1 Cor. 11:3; Eph. 5:21–23). What are your views about these verses and a husband's role as the head of the wife and the leader of the home?

8. Define leadership.

9. What does it not mean?

10. Who is responsible for the family's spiritual development? (Eph. 5:21–33; 1 Cor. 11:3)

11. What does God require concerning the character of the husband/spiritual leader? (2 Cor. 10:1; Gal. 5:22–23; 1 Thes. 2:7–8; 1 Tim. 3:1–10; 2 Tim. 2:24–25; Jas. 3:17–18)

Section 6 **Roles and Expectations**

12. Describe the husband's role as:

   a. Companion/friend _____
   _____
   _____
   _____

   b. Husband _____
   _____
   _____
   _____

   c. Provider _____
   _____
   _____
   _____

   d. Lover _____
   _____
   _____
   _____

   e. Father _____
   _____
   _____
   _____

   f. Disciplinarian _____
   _____
   _____
   _____

   g. Protector/guardian of the moral atmosphere of the home _____
   _____
   _____
   _____

Section 6 — Roles and Expectations

Wife's Role   (*To be answered by both*)

READ | Gen. 1:27   Gen. 2:18   Gen. 2:23–24   Eph. 5:33   Col. 3:18
1 Tim. 2:9–10   1 Tim. 3:11   1 Tim. 5:14   Titus 2:3–5   1 Pet. 3:1–7

13. What does Genesis 1:27 say about the woman's created status? _____
_____
_____

14. What do Genesis 2:18 and 2:23–24 say about a wife's role and equality? _____
_____
_____

15. What does 1 Peter 3:7 further say about a wife's equality? _____
_____
_____

16. What does it mean for the woman to be a helper or *help meet* (KJV)? (Gen. 2:18) _____
_____
_____
_____

17. What does God require concerning the character of the wife? (Eph. 5:33; 1 Tim. 2:9–10; 1 Tim. 3:11; Col. 3:18; Titus 2:3–5; 1 Pet. 3:1–5) _____
_____
_____
_____

18. Describe the woman's role as:

   a. Companion/friend _____
   _____
   _____

   b. Wife _____
   _____
   _____

Section 6 **Roles and Expectations**

    c. Lover _____
_____
_____

    d. Mother _____
_____
_____

    e. Disciplinarian _____
_____
_____

    f. Homemaker _____
_____
_____

    g. Protector/guardian of the moral atmosphere of the home _____
_____
_____

> ***So, I counsel younger widows to marry, to have children, to <u>manage their homes</u> and to give the enemy no opportunity for slander.*** (1 Tim. 5:14)

Note → **A. Noun** oikodespotes 3617, "a master of a house" (oikos, "a house," **despotes**, "a master"), is rendered "master of the house" in Matt. 10:25; Luke 13:25, and 14:21, where the context shows that the authority of the "householder" is stressed; **B. Verb**. oikodespoteo 3616, corresponding to A, "to rule a house," is used in 1 Tim. 5:14, RV, "rule the household" (KJV, "guide the house"). *Vine's Expository Dictionary of Biblical Words*

> *Since God assigns home management as the woman's area of responsibility, that responsibility requires appropriate authority. First Timothy 5:14 says that women are to "manage their homes." The word "manage" literally means," **to be house despot**," or total ruler. Some, unfortunately, teach biblical submission in such a restrictive way that the woman's responsibility remains, but the needed authority to accomplish it is removed.*[2]

19. Comment on the definition of the Greek word translated as the phrase "*manage their home.*" How do you see this applying to your relationship and to your household?
_____
_____
_____
_____

---

[2] Vickie Kraft, *Women Mentoring Women* (Chicago: Moody Publishing, 1992) 32-33. Used with permission.

Section 6 — Roles and Expectations

SUBMISSION

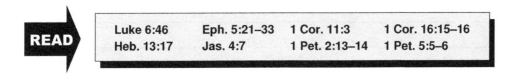

| Luke 6:46 | Eph. 5:21–33 | 1 Cor. 11:3 | 1 Cor. 16:15–16 |
| Heb. 13:17 | Jas. 4:7 | 1 Pet. 2:13–14 | 1 Pet. 5:5–6 |

A few thoughts about leadership, submission, and a controlling, abusive personality.

The husband is the head of the wife, and the wife is to submit to her husband (Eph. 5:22–24). Leadership, however, does not mean that a man does his own thing without consideration for his wife and family. A godly leader is a servant, not a dictator or king. The responsibility of the man is to lay down his life for his wife and family. Nowhere does God support the idea of a man lording it over his wife and leading in a dictatorial manner. Pastors and counselors hear two common complaints from women. One is that the husband is abusive and domineering, and the other is that he is passive and will not assume spiritual leadership.

Spousal abuse is a problem within the church. Christian women are seeking counseling because of abusive husbands—men who claim to be Christians and are often thought well of within their local church. Biblical references such as Ephesians 5:22 have generated a lot of teaching (and confusion and heartache) on the subject of submission. Some men twist Scripture to justify dominating and controlling their wives. Scriptures are used out of context and out of the character and example of Jesus Christ. Skewed teaching emphasizes the wife submitting to her husband but does not emphasize the husband gently loving and serving his wife as Christ loved and served the Church and gave Himself (suffered and died) for it. (John 3:16; Eph. 5:25).

On the other hand, to be fair, during the last four decades, men have been beaten down by society. Men have legitimate needs and feelings that have been marginalized, ignored, and mocked. As one popular speaker has explained, men have a fundamental need for respect, but, in many cases, they get little or no respect from their spouses.[3] Additionally, sometimes the woman is the abuser. In these cases, it is usually with mental, emotional, and verbal abuse. Wives can devastate their husbands with such things as undermining words and tone of voice, mental or emotional defiance, manipulation and control, nagging, belittling, sexual neglect, sexual manipulation, and control.

A dominating, controlling person might be one who dominates conversation or thoughts and feelings. In extreme personalities, it can lead to controlling every movement and to physical, mental, emotional, and sexual abuse. An abusive controlling man, for example, might overpower his spouse with spirituality—with words and superior Bible knowledge. During your dating and engagement, you might admire this as a sign of confidence and of capable leadership, and you might view it as a complement to your submissive, quiet, acquiescent nature. It might, however, be abuse wrapped in spiritual garb.

The next few pages contain questions about your views, feelings, and concerns about submission, leadership, authority, and controlling personalities.

---

[3] Emerson Eggerichs, *Love and Respect* DVD series. http://www.loveandrespect.com

Section 6 **Roles and Expectations**

1. Define submission. What does it mean? _____
   _____
   _____
   _____

2. What does it *not* mean? _____
   _____
   _____
   _____

3. To whom should the husband initially submit? (Luke 6:46; 1 Cor. 11:3; Jas. 4:7) _____
   _____
   _____
   _____

4. Does Ephesians 5:21 include mutual submission of the husband and wife to one another? What are your thoughts? _____
   _____
   _____

5. What does it mean to be in submission to those in authority over you? (1 Cor. 16:15–16; Heb. 13:17; 1 Pet. 5:5–6) _____
   _____
   _____
   _____

6. How are you in submission to those in spiritual authority? _____
   _____
   _____
   _____

7. To whom does God say the wife is to submit initially? (Luke 6:46; Jas. 4:7) _____
   _____

8. According to Ephesians 5:21–22, to whom should the wife submit? _____
   _____

Section 6   *Roles and Expectations*

9. What thoughts and feelings do you have about all the verses and teaching on submission? _____
   _____
   _____
   _____
   _____

10. Are there indications of a controlling personality in you? _____ If so, explain. _____
    _____
    _____
    _____
    _____

11. Are there indications of a controlling personality in your fiancé(e)? _____ If so, explain. _____
    _____
    _____
    _____
    _____

12. **(Man)** How will you fill the role of leadership? _____
    _____
    _____
    _____

13. **(Man)** Assuming your decisions do not go against the Bible, how will you respond if your wife disagrees with them and does not want to go along with them? _____
    _____
    _____
    _____
    _____

14. **(Both)** What should a husband do when his wife's choices, behavior, or demands are in opposition to the Bible? _____
    _____
    _____
    _____

Section 6   *Roles and Expectations*

Section 6   ***Roles and Expectations***

15. **(Woman)** How will you fulfill the role of a wife regarding submission to your husband? _____
_____
_____
_____
_____

16. **(Woman)** Assuming your husband's decisions do not go against the Bible, how will you respond to his leadership if you disagree with such things as his style of leadership, decisions, goals, vision, way of disciplining children, etc.? _____
_____
_____
_____
_____

17. **(Both)** What should a wife do if her husband's choices, behavior, or demands are in opposition to the Bible? _____
_____
_____
_____

18. **(Both)** Are you the type of man or woman who will be strong and stand up to guard the marriage, the home, and the children from all forms of ungodliness and abuse, and have boundaries for what is acceptable and conformable to love and holiness? _____
_____
_____
_____
_____

19. **(Both)** Are you the type of man or woman who, for fear of rejection or losing the relationship, or because of a desire to keep the peace, will shirk your responsibility and role, look the other way, or give in to unloving demands or to behaviors that are immoral, abusive, and ungodly? Comment:
_____
_____
_____
_____

Section 6 — Roles and Expectations

LIFESTYLE EXPECTATIONS

Planning is at the root of all successful endeavors. This is true whether in areas such as starting a business, building a house, landscaping a yard, or more to your immediate situation, planning your wedding. Can you imagine not planning your wedding ceremony? Imagine just showing up on the day and saying to the official, "Okay, we're here! Let's have the wedding!" That might work if you go to the courthouse to be married before a judge. However, even that would probably require minimal planning such as booking a time slot.

Some people plan their lives in a highly detailed manner. They have their objectives clearly lined out and proceed on course to accomplish all their plans. On the other hand, some people take life as it comes. And that's okay too. We all eventually make it to the other end of life and depart the world whether we planned our lives or not. It is also true that the best-laid plans do not always succeed. Life throws us many curves that alter and frustrate our efforts to succeed on a certain course. There is always the remote chance of winning the lottery or getting an inheritance, but aside from such happenstance, you don't build much of anything without planning and effort. Here are some major lifestyle categories that involve planning, discussion, and negotiation.

- Spiritual
- Careers
- Finances
- Possessions
- Housing
- Location
- Children/family
- Family etiquette
- Family roles and customs
- Recreation/vacations
- Social life
- Entertainment

1. Explain your agreement about double or single careers/jobs/income. [4] _____
   _____
   _____

2. Explain your agreement about where you will live (city, state, near or away from family). _____
   _____
   _____

3. Explain your agreement about housing (style, price, and location). _____
   _____
   _____

4. Are you in agreement about pets? _____ Will dogs, cats, or other animals be allowed in your house? _____ Are your families' attitudes about pets similar? _____

5. Explain your agreement about recreational activities and expenditures for such things. _____
   _____
   _____
   _____

---

[4] The section on finances covers these issues further.

Section 6 *Roles and Expectations*

6. What are your goals for the next five years? _____
   _____
   _____
   _____

7. What specific steps are you taking to achieve these goals? _____
   _____
   _____
   _____

8. What are your mid-range goals (5–10 years)? _____
   _____
   _____

9. What are your long-range goals (10–20 years)? _____
   _____
   _____

10. Comment on how you share the same goals and vision for each phase of your marriage. _____
    _____
    _____
    _____

11. Comment on how you agree about finances (income, spending, debt, credit cards, savings, and investments). _____
    _____
    _____
    _____

12. Any other comments about goals and planning? _____
    _____
    _____
    _____

Section 6 — Roles and Expectations

HOLIDAY EXPECTATIONS

Christmas, Thanksgiving, and Easter

As a newly married couple, how will you spend your first Thanksgiving, your first Christmas, and perhaps every family holiday after that? If you are a couple in your early twenties, you are somewhat fresh out of the nest. Until now, you have most likely spent Christmas and Thanksgiving with your own family, and it has been a warm time with fond memories and traditions. Now you have two sets of parents to consider, and each may hope you spend it with them.

You have probably seen movies in which this scenario is played out Hollywood style, i.e. the relationship of a sweet and happy newlywed couple is severely tested with fights, hurt feelings, and estrangement over family holidays—only to be wonderfully resolved in 1½ hours! For some couples, such a scenario is reality (except for the 1½–hour resolve time!)

It is discomforting to make choices between loved ones on such occasions, and it might be this way for you until you become parents and begin to develop your own family holiday events.

Sometimes the question is not only where you will spend holidays but also *how* you will spend them. You may have different styles of doing Christmas. One, for example, may think Christmas is pagan—no trees or presents allowed! The other may get ecstatic over decorating a tree with a zillion ornaments, piling gifts to the ceiling, and leaving cookies out for Santa Claus! Likewise, Easter can be a time of purely celebrating Christ's resurrection, or it can be a time of little or no spiritual content—a time of chocolate bunnies and Easter egg hunts. So, what do you do? Let's find out!

1. Describe your family's (or your) style of celebrating:

    Thanksgiving: _____
    _____
    _____
    _____

    Christmas: _____
    _____
    _____
    _____

    Easter: _____
    _____
    _____
    _____

2. Where will you, as a couple, spend your first Thanksgiving?_____

    Your first Christmas? _____

Section 6   ***Roles and Expectations***

3. How will you handle subsequent family holidays? _____
   _____
   _____
   _____

4. Do you anticipate issues or problems with your parents over your holiday choices? _____ Explain
   _____
   _____
   _____

5. How important is it to celebrate Christmas with a tree and all the lights, decorations, stockings, etc.?
                                           (Circle)   Very   Moderately   Not at all

6. How important is gift giving at Christmas?   Very   Moderately   Not at all

7. Do you want to celebrate Christmas with a manger scene and other biblical depictions? _____
   Santa Claus and reindeer? _____

8. Will you promote Santa Claus (even as pretend time) to your children? _____ What are your views on promoting the Santa Claus story to children? _____
   _____
   _____

Halloween

9. Explain your views about Halloween. _____
   _____
   _____
   _____

10. Will you let your kids dress in costumes and go trick-or-treating? _____
    If so, what kind of costumes will you permit? _____
    _____

11. What are your views about attending a church-sponsored event on Halloween? _____
    _____
    _____
    _____

Section 6   **Roles and Expectations**

Anniversaries & birthdays

12. How important is celebrating anniversaries? (Circle)   Very   Moderately   Not at all

    How important is gift giving on anniversaries?   Very   Moderately   Not at all

    How important is celebrating birthdays?   Very   Moderately   Not at all

    How important is gift giving on birthdays?   Very   Moderately   Not at all

13. Explain how you want to celebrate anniversaries. _____

    _____

    _____

    _____

    _____

14. Explain how you want to celebrate birthdays. _____

    _____

    _____

    _____

    _____

15. If you have differences regarding holidays and other special occasions, how are you resolving these differences? _____

    _____

    _____

    _____

    _____

    _____

Parting thoughts about anniversaries

For women, more so it seems than for some men, anniversaries are special occasions full of meaning and importance, and women want their spouses to remember their anniversary without any hints. Women look forward to special treatment on these occasions—flowers, intimate, thoughtful gifts such as jewelry or perfume (not cookware or vacuum cleaners), dinner at a nice restaurant, and other such things. Women want to know that they are deeply loved and esteemed. Anniversaries are a time when the expectation for such affirmation is at its highest. It behooves a husband to know his wife in this matter. Women can be wounded easily and deeply by careless neglect and forgetfulness in this area. Moreover, the wounds and pain can stay within them a very, very long time—even years.

Section 6 — Roles and Expectations

FAMILY PLANNING

Jesus used common examples from nature to illustrate many aspects and attributes of God and of the Kingdom of God. For example, God has built the law of exponential growth into every species of plant and animal (Gen. 26:12; Matt. 13:8; 19:29). It is beyond comprehension how a tiny seed can become a tree that bears thousands of apples. It's as mysterious as it is astounding that one small, insignificant cone or pine nut can become a giant tree two hundred feet tall and weighing 1000 tons.[5] Considering the diminutive size of a cone makes it seem impossible.

But even more astounding is how two microscopic particles of substance can merge, begin to replicate, and be self-directed to form highly complex, highly specialized body parts that become a human being. It's the mysterious power and miracle we call *life*.

Life is wonderful. Even with all the pain, sorrow, and tragedy, life is good and life is awesome. What does all this have to do with family? God said to be fruitful and multiply (Gen. 1:28). In addition to the joys of parenthood, having children is an expression of faith, obedience, love, and gratitude to God. The desire to have children is the desire to honor life and to honor God. The desire to have children is a declaration that God is good, that life is good, and that life is worth it. The desire to have children is an expression of faith—faith in God, faith in life, and faith in the processes of life.

We live in an extremely self-absorbed culture. Because of a trend among some couples, a strange acronym (DINK) has come into usage. It stands for **D**ouble **I**ncome **N**o **K**ids. I suppose the translation of this mindset is something like the following: *Kids are a hassle. The world is too ugly and brutal a place to raise kids—they're better off not being born. We can't afford to have kids. Pregnancy is ugly, and it will ruin my (or my wife's) beautiful svelte body—don't want that to happen! Kids end up breaking your heart anyhow . . . so who needs that?*

Not only does such reasoning betray self-centeredness, it also betrays a lack of faith, love, and obedience to God. This is not to say that every couple should produce children in a robotic way to fill a divine mandate or quota. It's just to say that much of what passes for sophisticated, logical, family *un*-planning might instead be self-centered, self-indulgent thinking.

Furthermore, contrary to what some believe, a pregnant woman is a beautiful sight. Why? Because it is *life happening*. It's creation on parade. Granted, for you women, the prospect of gaining weight and having your body stretched out of shape is not glamorous. But, there is loveliness that is far more attractive than glamour. Aside from the discomfort, pain, and physical changes it brings, pregnancy is immensely beautiful.

In short: life is worth it. Children are worth it! They are worth all the pain and self-denial that it will take to get them to adulthood—and even after that, it's not always a pleasure cruise. But life is worth it.

> *And God blessed them, and God said unto them, Be fruitful, and multiply, and replenish the earth.* (Gen. 1:28)

God's first blessing to Adam and Eve was . . . *children*.

---

[5] From the Web site: www.americanparknetwork.com

Section 6 — Roles and Expectations

1. When you look at children, or when you consider the prospect of having your own, do you think of them as a blessing? _____

2. What words come to mind with the thought of having your own children? _____
   _____
   _____

3. Are children a part of your plans for life together? _____
   When? _____ How many? _____ How far between? _____

4. Are you thrilled by the prospect of being a mommy or daddy? _____

5. One a scale of 1–5, how much are you looking forward to eventually having children? _____

6. Write a few lines about your desire or lack of desire for children. _____
   _____
   _____
   _____

7. a. What thoughts and feelings does pregnancy bring to your mind? _____
      _____
      _____

   b. What goes through your mind when you see a pregnant woman? _____
      _____
      _____

8. Are you nurturing by nature? _____ Do you want to nurture children? _____

9. If you don't want children, are you and your fiancé(e) in complete agreement about that? _____
   Explain_____
   _____
   _____

10. Are you in agreement about the type of education you want for your children? _____

11. Will they be educated in: Public? _____ Private? _____ Home school? _____ College? ____

12. Are you in agreement about the style of discipline for your children? _____ Explain _____
    _____
    _____

Section 6 — Roles and Expectations

13. Will you be a stay-at-home mother? _____   A stay-at-home father? _____

14. Will you put your children in day care? _____

15. Do you believe a day care or a caretaker is an okay substitute so you can pursue your career? _____

16. Give your thoughts on day care or other caretakers for your children. _____
    _____
    _____

17. Are you in agreement about contraception—the idea of it as well as the method? _____

18. If you can't have children, will you adopt? _____   Would you seek a surrogate? _____

19. How often do you interact with children? ☐ Never   ☐ Occasionally   ☐ Often   ☐ A lot

20. Where are you in the birth order of your siblings? # _____ out of # _____ siblings.

21. Were you a primary or frequent caregiver for your younger siblings? If so, how might this influence your outlook on, or your desire for, children? _____
    _____
    _____

22. a. Do you interact with children now? _____ Whose children? _____

    b. Describe your interaction with children _____
    _____
    _____

    c. Describe your fiancé(e)'s interaction with children _____
    _____
    _____

23. If you have suffered or perpetrated molestation or abuse of any kind, or have had an abortion, how might this affect your interaction with children (either yours or another's)? Explain:
    _____
    _____
    _____
    _____

Section 6 — Roles and Expectations

SOCIAL LIFE

1. What do you like to do for social life? _____
   _____
   _____

2. What does your fiancé(e) like to do? _____
   _____
   _____

3. List social activities you like to do together.
   _____   _____
   _____   _____
   _____   _____

4. Are you interested in your fiancé(e)'s friends? ___ Is your (fiancé(e) interested in your friends?___

5. Do you foresee having to give up any current relationships once you are married? _____
   If so, which ones and why? _____
   _____
   _____

6. Do you have concerns about any of your fiancé(e)'s associations or friendships? _____
   _____
   _____

7. Does your fiancé(e) have concerns about any of your associations or friendships? _____ Comment:
   _____
   _____

8. Do you have friends within the faith? _____ Are they mutual friends? _____ Do you relate well with them? _____ Do your friends influence you toward godliness? _____ Do they influence you away from God? _____

9. When you interact with your friends or associates, do you leave Jesus at home? _____

10. Do you expect to be able to keep close, personal friendships with opposite-gender friends? Comment
    _____
    _____

Section 6   **Roles and Expectations**

11. Do you have opposite-gender friends that you want to keep but who would make your spouse uncomfortable? _____ Who are they? _____

12. Does your fiancé(e) have opposite-gender friends that he or she wants to keep and does not understand your uncomfortable feelings? _____ Who are these friends? _____

13. Would you resent having to give up these friendships? _____ Comment _____

14. Do either of you have opposite-gender Internet relationships? _____ If they are not your spouse's mutual friends, will you end these relationships? _____

15. a. Other than your fiancé(e), with whom do you share your personal struggles? _____

    b. How deep is this sharing? _____

    c. Is the sharing mutual? _____

16. Do you share your relationship *with your fiancé(e)* with anyone? _____ If so, with whom and why?

17. What aspects of your social life would you like to be different? _____

Section 7 *Communication*

COMMUNICATION

Many elements go into making a healthy, godly relationship. One's personal faith in Jesus Christ and wholehearted reception of grace and redemption is the foundation for our relationships. A Christian couple is first brother and sister in the Lord and then husband and wife in the Lord. This means you have the same spiritual "language," which is the prerequisite for communication in a godly relationship. Our common faith gives us that essential spiritual relationship and language base. The issue then becomes communicating within the common language of faith as brother and sister and as husband and wife.

Just as blood carries nutrients to the cells and carries oxygen to the brain, so does communication and understanding carry all the elements of health to every fiber of your relationship. Perhaps you have heard that statement so often it has become monotonous. Yet, a major complaint—perhaps the foremost complaint—from spouses is lack of communication.

Communication goes on all the time whether you, as a couple, consciously attempt it or not. For example, a message is being sent when a husband gives his wife of thirty years a look that says, *You're still the only one.* On the other hand, he sends a different message when he ignores his wife's desire for attention in favor of watching TV. He is saying she's not important to him right now. Wives can convey very powerful messages in nonverbal ways. With just a look from across the room at a crowded corporate event, a woman can tell her husband he is more man than all the rest put together. Conversely, disrespect and disdain for one's husband can be said with a mere facial expression. Nonverbal communications say a lot. In fact, various sources say that words make up as little as 7 to 10 percent of communication while tone of voice and body language make up a much greater percentage. Verbal or otherwise, whether we know it or not, we are constantly communicating with each other. The only question is, *What's the message?*

In order to have a healthy marriage relationship, communication has to be effective. It is easy to understand someone when the talk is external. *Bring me the bucket of red paint that is next to the ladder* is a very specific message. However, *that door is going to fall off its hinges one of these days,* or *maybe you should think about wearing a different dress* are statements without a clear message and are subject to the recipient's interpretation. Thus, effective communication means understanding a message in its intended meaning.

Men and women communicate differently. There are many resources available to help you learn about these differences.[1] In order to have a good relationship, you will want to understand your different modes of communication and make adjustments for these differences. Otherwise, like the title of a 2003 movie, your relationship will be *Lost in Translation*. The following section is a survey to see how you are doing in the communication department.

---

[1] For example, the *Love and Respect* video series by Emerson Eggerichs is a powerful presentation on understanding your mate and on communication between husband and wife.

Section 7   *Communication*

The lighter side of communication

Sally Forth / by Greg Howard
SALLY FORTH © KING FEATURES SYNDICATE Used by permission

Section 7 — Communication

COMMUNICATION INVENTORY

On a scale of 1–5, rate your level of agreement with the following statements. Then rate what you think is your fiancé(e)'s level of agreement with the statements.

　　1 = Very poor, never, totally disagree with statement
　　2 = Poor, almost never, mostly disagree with statement
　　3 = So-so, average, not sure, sometimes agree or disagree with the statement
　　4 = Good, often, mostly agree with statement
　　5 = Excellent, always, totally agree with statement

Examples:　#1　The quality of our communication is . . .
　　　　　　　Give your rating of communication between the two of you, and then what you think your fiancé(e)'s rating will be.
　　　　　　#3　I listen to my fiancé(e) and sincerely seek to understand her/him.
　　　　　　　Rate how well you do this and then how well your fiancé(e) does this.

	You	Your Fiancé(e)
1. The quality of our communication is	___	___
2. The quantity of our communication is	___	___
3. I listen to my fiancé(e) and sincerely seek to understand her/him.	___	___
4. I refrain from predicting what my fiancé(e) is going to say.	___	___
5. I interrupt when my fiancé(e) is talking.	___	___
6. I generally think the best about a person's motives.	___	___
7. I generally think the worst about a person's motives.	___	___
8. I generally think the best about people.	___	___
9. I pay attention when someone is speaking; I don't let my mind wander.	___	___
10. When confronted about a bad trait, I don't withdraw or get defensive.	___	___
11. I joyfully accept correction or reproof that is given in genuine concern.	___	___
12. I humbly correct people. I seek their well-being and not my own rightness.	___	___
13. When we disagree, I first seek to understand my fiancé(e)'s point of view.	___	___
14. When my fiancé(e) and I differ in spiritual matters, I am generally right.	___	___
15. I think my fiancé(e) is more spiritual than I am.	___	___
16. I think my fiancé(e)'s opinions are generally better than mine are.	___	___
17. I gossip or talk negatively about people behind their backs.	___	___
18. I use anger as a means to control and dominate.	___	___
19. I use tears, crying, or depression as a means to control and dominate.	___	___

Section 7 — Communication

	You	Your Fiancé(e)
20. I seek to uplift my fiancé(e) in everything I say and do.		
21. I pray a blessing on my fiancé(e) daily.		
22. I seek to protect my fiancé(e) when he or she is wounded or vulnerable.		
23. I verbally give appreciation, admiration, and respect to my fiancé(e)		
24. I say, "I love you" often to my fiancé(e) and mean it wholeheartedly.		
25. I speak respectfully and admiringly of my fiancé(e) to others.		
26. When he/she is clearly wrong, I confront my fiancé(e) firmly yet gently.		
27. I say what I think others want to hear. I am a people pleaser.		
28. I have difficulty saying the words "I love you."		
29. I like witty sarcasm and/or little put-downs. I think they are fun and cute.		
30. I communicate respect to my fiancé(e) often and in various ways.		
31. I like hearing the words "I love you."		
32. I share things spoken to me in confidence.		
33. I share things about others that put them in an unfavorable light.		
34. I use the time someone is speaking to prepare my rebuttal. I am more interested in countering with my opinion.		
35. I often say, "I love you" in nonverbal ways via eye contact, helping, thoughtful consideration, gifts, etc.		
36. When another person is talking, I interrupt to correct or to voice my opinions.		
37. I apologize too quickly (as a means to divert attention from my issues or to stop conversation.)		
38. I withhold my thoughts, opinions, corrections, etc. for fear of rejection, disapproval, or conflict. (5 means you always withhold.)		

Section 7 — Communication

WHAT'S YOUR LOVE LANGUAGE?

Communication has a lot to do with the mutual exchange of the various forms of intimacy. In this area, as always, understanding your spouse is the key. Learning your mate's *love language*—a concept popularized by Gary Chapman—is one way you can enhance your communication. The concept is not explicitly and solidly supported in scripture. (It can be inferred in verses such as 1 Pet 3:7 ...*husbands dwell with your wives* **in an understanding way**.) Nevertheless, the concept does have merit as it is borne out in experiences between couples.

The gist of this concept is that people have different ways they perceive they are being loved and different ways they express their love. According to Chapman, we typically express love to our spouse in the language we want it expressed to us, and thereby miss the target. If you express love to your spouse in a way that he or she doesn't want or need it to be expressed, then no matter how good your intentions, the message your spouse will get is that you do not love him or her. It's a simple concept but one that you might easily brush aside.

> **Suggested assignment**
> *The Five Love Languages*
> by Gary Chapman

Marriage can be likened to taking dance lessons. Good dancers practice a lot. They come to the place where they know their partner's every move, and when on the dance floor, they seem to move together effortlessly—just like they were made for each other. Marriage, like dancing, takes a lot of practice. It takes a lot of trial and error and adjustments. Becoming great dancers or, in our case great lovers, is worth the effort because marriage is very rewarding. Therefore, in this section, we want to look at the way you express love and the way you want love expressed to you. It's part of the dance. Read Chapman's book to have the full idea before doing the following exercise.

Chapman lists five love languages: (1) Words of Affirmation (2) Giving/Receiving Gifts (3) Quality Time (4) Acts of Service (5) Physical Touch. The survey below expands on these five love languages to help you have a clearer understanding of the one that most describes your style.

1. Using the numbers 1–10, prioritize the ways you like to express love and get a sense of being loved. For example, if letter "g" (being emotionally connected) is most important to you, put the number "1" next to "g," and then prioritize the rest.

   Note: In light of letters *e* and *f*, project your answers into the future, when you will be married.

   a. Verbal—expressing love and affirmation with words.

   b. Quality time – focusing attention on one another without distraction.

   c. Giving and receiving thoughtful gifts (large or small).

   d. Acts of service – helping with chores, fixing things, etc.

   e. Physical touch 1 – non-sexual hugs, snuggling, hand holding.

   f. Physical touch 2 – sex – being sexually interested and available.

   g. Being emotionally connected – tuned in to each other's feelings.

   h. Sharing ideas and opinions.

   i. Meeting material needs, providing income.

   j. Being mutually interested in hobbies, recreation, interests, etc.

Section 7 — Communication

It is important for you to pay attention to your fiancé(e)'s answers. If you are trying to please your fiancé(e) with the wrong love lingo—if you are not speaking his or her love language—you are apt to miss the dance, although your intentions are good. The solution is to express love in the way your partner perceives being loved—even if it is not the way you like to express or receive love. For example, (when married) if your wife likes to have her feet rubbed after she has worked hard all day, you had better rub her feet (not other body parts). Conversely, your husband's idea of significant touching may not be a foot rub. You get the picture!

For the man: Do you know what type of perfume your fiancée likes? Will you buy it for her? (Never mind that it costs $80.00 a bottle.) Does she like you to open doors for her? Does she like lots of hugs (i.e., nonsensuous, nonsexual touching)? Do you give her lots of hugs, or would she say that you don't hug her enough?

For the woman: Do you admire him? Do you express your admiration of him? Do you respect his opinions and voice your respect? Are you proud of him, and does he sense this from you? Do you know his hobbies or interests and have at least some interest in them if he wants you to?

Below are some questions for your consideration. Again, since you are not married yet, there are boundaries (there should be) to your physical expressions of love. When answering, you may want to project your thinking forward to when you *are* married so that you and your fiancé(e) can have a clearer idea of your needs, desires, and what each may expect.

2. What is your fiancé(e)'s primary love language? _____

3. On a scale of 1–5, how well (and how often) do you speak your fiancé(e)'s love language? _____

4. When I am depressed, blue, down, I want my fiancé(e) to _____

5. When I get into self-pity, I want my fiancé(e) to _____

6. I wish my fiancé(e) would more frequently _____

7. I know that my fiancé(e) loves me when he/she _____

8. What I really want from my fiancé(e) is _____

9. I get a sense of comfort when my fiancé(e) _____

Section 7　　　　　　　　　　　　　　　　　　　　　　　　　　　*Communication*

10. When I want to show my fiancé(e) love, I (or I will when we are married) _____
   _____
   _____
   _____

11. When I want my fiancé(e) to show me love, I want him/her (or when we are married) to _____
   _____
   _____
   _____

12. What I like *best* about my fiancé(e) is _____
   _____
   _____
   _____

13. What I like *least* about my fiancé(e) is _____
   _____
   _____
   _____

14. What I like *best* about myself is _____
   _____
   _____
   _____

15. What I like *least* about myself is _____
   _____
   _____
   _____

16. My greatest fear is _____
   _____
   _____

17. My fiancé(e)'s greatest fear is _____
   _____

Section 7 — Communication

RESOLVING CONFLICTS

Gen. 3:11–13	Gen. 13:7–12	Ps. 51:6	Ps. 66:18	Prov. 17:14
Prov. 18:13	Prov. 20:3	Matt. 5:23–25	Matt. 6:14–15	Matt. 7:3–5, 12
Matt. 15:18–20	Matt. 18:15–17	Mark 7:20–23	Luke 11:13	John 13:15
Rom. 5:8	Gal. 5:19–26	Eph. 4:22–32	Phil. 3:13–14	Heb. 8:12
Heb. 10:24	Jas. 1:13–25	Jas. 4:1–11	Jas. 5:16	

One pastor who does a lot of premarital counseling asks engaged couples if they have had any disagreements, conflicts, or fights. If they haven't had any, he advises them to go home and have one. And he is serious![2] If you have never had a conflict, disagreement, fight, argument, hurt feelings, or anything else of the sort in your relationship, it is cause for consideration. Either you are two very devoted souls, or you are two very delusional souls!

Adjusting to each other's personality, mannerisms, habits, and quirks is a normal part of the process of becoming one. Maybe you have already experienced minor offenses that do not cause much conflict. Whether large or small, you must accept that problems in your relationship will occur. In fact, we might go so far as to say that conflict is not an indicator of the health of your relationship, but how you resolve conflict surely is. You may choose to view disagreements, hard times, trials, problems, and such things as signs of having chosen the wrong mate, or you may choose to view them as opportunities to examine and improve your love for, and commitment to, God and to your fiancé(e). Problems in your relationship are *your* opportunities to grow; they are *your* opportunities to die to self.

The source of conflicts

Conflicts often occur simply because a couple does not have the knowledge and skill to communicate well. They don't understand the fundamental and valid differences between the male mind and the female mind. These differences must be understood and accepted. Otherwise, your relationship will suffer, and conflicts will occur more readily and remain unresolved.

In addition to the differences between male and female thought processes, conflict can spring from childhood upbringing and environment—how your families dealt with miscommunication and conflicts vs. how your fiancé(e)'s family did. Another major factor is your personality. Are you aggressive, dominant, self-assured, or are you passive, reserved, acquiescent, and submissive? Do you run away from conflicts or do you head straight into conflicts and try to resolve them?

Other than ignorance and lack of communication skills, there are a couple of other sources of conflicts. Ultimately, conflicts occur because of sin, the hardness of our hearts, and our old nature. Another source, which must not be overlooked, is our enemy, Satan. Jesus specifically emphasizes the reality of the devil. We have an enemy in the spirit realm. However, in our day-to-day relationships, Jesus makes it clear that most of our problems emanate from our own hearts (Matt. 15:18–20; Mark 7:20–23). Paul reiterates this in Galatians 5:19–26.

---

[2] Thanks to Pastor Steve Carr for material on resolving conflicts. For many more resources, visit his Web site at www.covenantkeepers.org

Section 7 **Communication**

The devil made me do it.

Years ago, I heard a joke that went something like this:

> The devil was sitting on a curb crying. Someone walked up to him and said, "What's the matter, Devil? Why are you crying?" The devil replied through sad tears, "Aw, those Christians are always blaming me for stuff I never got a chance to do."

Some Christians blame the devil for almost every conflict and problem in their lives. If they are having problems with their spouse, it's because demons are behind it. For them, the way to deal with the situation is to do warfare against the devil by casting out or rebuking demons and demonic influence. Often, there is no healing and no fruit. In fact, more damage is done to the relationship. Why? It's because the devil most likely is not the problem.

1. From the list of verses on the previous page, what is the cause of conflict? _____
   _____
   _____

2. From where does strife emanate? (Matt. 15:19–20; Jas. 4:1) _____
   _____
   _____

3. Do these Scriptures lay the cause and blame on the devil or demons? _____

4. Where does Scripture place the fault? _____
   _____
   _____

5. Look up James 4:7–8 (KJV) and fill in the blanks.

   vs. 7 Therefore _____ _____ to God. _____ the devil and he will _____ from you. **vs. 8** _____ _____ to God and He will draw near to you. Cleanse your hands, you sinners; and purify _____ _____ you double-minded.

6. Look up James 5:16 and fill in the blanks.

   Confess your (*your own*) _____ to one another, and _____ for one another, that you may be healed. The effective, fervent prayer of a righteous man avails much.

> **NOTE:** We are to confess **our own** faults (not our mate's faults). Much conflict and pain can be avoided if you will acknowledge your part in the problem. Often, we would rather focus on our mate's issues, but if you will acknowledge **your** own sin**, your** own fault, and **your** own weakness, and not try to justify yourself, you will find the healing that often escapes couples who point fingers at one another.

Section 7 — Communication

CONFLICT RESOLUTION INVENTORY

Rate yourself and your fiancé(e) on the quality of your conflict resolution.
(Adapted from the article *How to Resolve Conflicts in a Biblical Way*—Steve Carr. Used with permission)

Circle the number that reflects your level of agreement. Place an X over the number that you think applies to your fiancé(e). If it's the same, circle and X the same number.

← Disagree | Agree →

	Totally Disagree	Mildly Disagree	Not Sure 50/50	Mildly Agree	Totally Agree
1. We never have conflicts, disagreements, or differing views	1	2	3	4	5
2. We occasionally have conflicts, disagreements, or differing views	1	2	3	4	5
3. We often have conflicts, disagreements, or differing views	1	2	3	4	5
4. I seek to avoid conflicts, disagreements.	1	2	3	4	5
5. Conflicts make me uncomfortable. I can't handle conflict.	1	2	3	4	5
6. Conflicts are signs of relational distancing.	1	2	3	4	5
7. Conflicts do not frighten me. I am not threatened by conflicts.	1	2	3	4	5
8. I'm afraid of having arguments with my fiancé(e).	1	2	3	4	5

When in conflict with my fiancé(e):

9. I plow ahead into the conflict and seek a solution.	1	2	3	4	5
10. I pull back and withdraw from conflict—hoping to keep the peace.	1	2	3	4	5
11. I embrace the conflict with a competitive spirit seeking to win.	1	2	3	4	5
12. I acquiesce to my fiancé(e) as a means of avoiding rejection.	1	2	3	4	5
13. I acquiesce to my fiancé(e); winning is just not that important.	1	2	3	4	5
14. I acquiesce but secretly hold bitterness, sorrow, or other emotions.	1	2	3	4	5
15. I pass the blame onto my fiancé(e). (Gen. 3:11–13)	1	2	3	4	5
16. I insist on facing the issue immediately.	1	2	3	4	5
17. I deal fairly with my fiancé(e) when conflicts arise.	1	2	3	4	5
18. I actively seek reconciliation after a conflict. (Matt. 5:23–25; 18:15)	1	2	3	4	5
19. I seek reconciliation quickly. (Matt. 5:25; Eph. 4:26)	1	2	3	4	5
20. I am completely honest about the facts of the conflict. (Ps. 51:6)	1	2	3	4	5
21. I restrain my anger during a conflict. (Prov. 20:3; 17:14)	1	2	3	4	5

Section 7 — Communication

	Totally Disagree	Mildly Disagree	Not Sure 50/50	Mildly Agree	Totally Agree
22. I allow my fiancé(e) and myself some cooling off time to collect our thoughts and consider why we were so affected.	1	2	3	4	5
23. I seek to listen to and understand what my fiancé(e) thinks when a disagreement occurs. (Prov. 18:13; Jas. 1:19)	1	2	3	4	5
24. After we have had an argument, I humble myself and confess my fault first. (Gen. 3:11–13; Matt. 7:5; Jas. 5:16)	1	2	3	4	5
25. I forgive and refuse to bring the issue up again. (Ps. 66:18; Matt. 6:14–15; Eph. 4:31–32; Phil. 3:13; Heb. 8:12)	1	2	3	4	5
26. I tell my fiancé(e), in love, specifically what action or attitudes I want to see change. (Matt. 18:15)	1	2	3	4	5
27. We keep talking until we reach a mutually agreed upon compromise. (Gen. 13:7–13)	1	2	3	4	5
28. I pray regularly for the grace to change. (Luke 11:13; Jas. 5:16)	1	2	3	4	5
29. I am patient and long-suffering when things do not change as quickly as I want. (Gal. 5:22–23)	1	2	3	4	5
30. I take specific action to change even when my fiancé(e) will not. (Matt. 7:3–5, 12; John 13:15; Rom. 5:8; Heb. 10:24)	1	2	3	4	5
31. When we have conflicts, I seek what my part in the problem is.	1	2	3	4	5
32. I am very willing to confess my fault, if such is the case.	1	2	3	4	5
33. I constantly work to develop and maintain our relationship via good communication practices.	1	2	3	4	5
34. I am more interested in loving my fiancé(e) and being kind to her/him than I am in being right or getting my way.	1	2	3	4	5
35. I accept our differences, and I don't try to change my fiancé(e).	1	2	3	4	5
36. I try to change my fiancé(e). (Matt. 7:3–5)	1	2	3	4	5
37. I wish my fiancé(e) would change in some areas.	1	2	3	4	5
38. I sincerely ask for forgiveness when I have wronged my fiancé(e).	1	2	3	4	5
39. I readily forgive my fiancé(e) when asked to. I don't keep the offense in my file box of debts owed to me. (Luke 17:4; Eph. 4:32; Heb. 8:12)	1	2	3	4	5
40. To forgive when I don't *feel* like forgiving would be hypocritical.	1	2	3	4	5
41. I honestly (completely) forgive whether I feel like it or not. (Ps. 78:38)	1	2	3	4	5

Section 7   *Communication*

ISSUES CHECKLIST

Note: Do this checklist together

Spend some time talking about each item and then circle the number that reflects the level of agreement you have as a couple.

Disagree ← / Agree →

	Totally Disagree	Mildly Disagree	Not sure 50/50	Mildly Agree	Totally Agree
1. Use of money – who will make the final decisions	1	2	3	4	5
2. Use of credit cards	1	2	3	4	5
3. Debt – repayment of debt	1	2	3	4	5
4. Major purchases (home, cars, furniture, luxury items such as vacations, snowmobiles, motorcycles)	1	2	3	4	5
5. General purchases (food, clothing, electronics, cosmetics, etc.)	1	2	3	4	5
6. Financial planning (income, savings, investments)	1	2	3	4	5
7. General lifestyle (well-appointed, modest, sparse, etc.)	1	2	3	4	5
8. Careers, job changes	1	2	3	4	5
9. Double or single careers or incomes	1	2	3	4	5
10. Amount of time at work	1	2	3	4	5
11. Entertainment (type, frequency, etc.)	1	2	3	4	5
12. Types of recreation – sports – pastimes	1	2	3	4	5
13. Amount of time devoted to sports, hobbies, pastimes	1	2	3	4	5
14. Family planning (use of contraceptives or not)	1	2	3	4	5
15. Children (if any, how many, how soon, etc.)	1	2	3	4	5
16. Stay at home mom, day care, or other childcare provider.	1	2	3	4	5
17. Family health (medical insurance, immunizations, etc.)	1	2	3	4	5
18. Family eating style (types of food, cooking)	1	2	3	4	5
19. Use of alcohol or drugs	1	2	3	4	5
20. Pets (what kind, how many, where they will sleep, etc.)	1	2	3	4	5
21. Friends, social life	1	2	3	4	5
22. Hanging out with the guys – gals (same gender)	1	2	3	4	5
23. Contact with opposite gender (former friends, dates, boy/girl friends, schoolmates, work colleagues, etc.	1	2	3	4	5

Section 7 — Communication

	Totally Disagree	Mildly Disagree	Not sure 50/50	Mildly Agree	Totally Agree
24. Time spent alone – time spent together	1	2	3	4	5
25. Showing affection (how, how often, when, where)	1	2	3	4	5
26. Dealing with in-laws	1	2	3	4	5
27. Sex in general—how, when, how often (more on this in another section)	1	2	3	4	5
28. Church attendance (where, when, how often)	1	2	3	4	5
29. Family devotions	1	2	3	4	5
30. Bible reading, prayer, worship	1	2	3	4	5
31. Tithing–giving money to church, missions, charities, etc.	1	2	3	4	5
32. Involvement in ministry (how, when, where, how much)	1	2	3	4	5
33. Spiritual vision (missionary work, etc.)	1	2	3	4	5
34. Male-female roles in religion/spiritual life	1	2	3	4	5
35. Male-female roles in general life (more in next section)	1	2	3	4	5

Little Foxes

One thing that causes misunderstanding and confusion is when one spouse has a habitual response pattern of becoming angry, frustrated, depressed, moody, or otherwise emotionally troubled over everyday problems and frustrations (for example, getting angry when having a problem changing a car's headlight or getting a computer to work correctly. ... Ugh!) These types of responses often are indicative of walking in the flesh and not in the spirit—perhaps doing things we think we *should* do but actually are not gifted or called *to* do. Sometimes these frustrations are indicative of deeper issues such as unresolved sin and self-condemnation in another area. They could be about feelings of bitterness or judgmental attitudes toward others that backfire.

In these situations, the other spouse is tempted to enter into his or her spouse's errant emotional issues. In other words, by reacting emotionally to the other's issue, one takes on that emotional problem and becomes entwined in it–thus increasing an already emotionally charged situation. This happens because the one spouse does not stand apart from the other's emotional state, but rather enters it—thinking, perhaps, that he or she must help fix the problem or change or correct the other. However, it is not his or her responsibility or ability to do so. The truth is each person must take ownership of his or her own emotional responses. The one who is angry or depressed, for example, must take ownership and responsibility for his/her emotions and not blame the other. The fact that your spouse pushes your buttons only demonstrates that you have reactive buttons (defensiveness) that can be pushed. When your spouse has such problems, you must stand back and realize that you are not the problem, the cause of the problem, or the solution to the problem.

Many times, the problem is not about glitches in computers and other similar frustrations. Often, it is relational discord. In this case, the person with anger (or moodiness, depression, or whatever the emotion) can, indeed, affect his or her spouse with unkind, hateful, inconsiderate, and deprecating words and attitudes. These assaults affect the other person greatly, and attack the oneness of the union. It is one thing to get angry or depressed about your car (although that's an issue to resolve); it is another thing to be angry or moody with your spouse. Your emotional outbursts or moods can't grieve your car one bit, but they can decimate your spouse. Even so, the offended person has a mandate from Scripture not to respond in kind. We are to return blessing for evil and to bless those who persecute us and treat us spitefully. (Matt. 5:44; Rom. 12:14; 1 Cor. 4:12; Rom. 12:20-21) This doesn't mean we have to take abuse and, thereby, let it control us. Yet, it does at least mean we should not become entangled in our spouse's errant emotions or be abusive in return.

> *Catch us the foxes, the little foxes that spoil the vines: for*
> *our vines have tender grapes.* (Song of Solomon 2:15)

It is the little offenses that gradually build up and turn our hearts away from each other. It's the little foxes that get in. It's the little offenses and disappointments—ignored and unresolved—that creep in day by day and spoil the fruit of passion and the vine of your relationship. Be on guard against the little foxes.

LOVE

This section is about 1 Corinthians chapter 13. In it, the apostle Paul clearly lays out what love really is. This kind of love is the only sure foundation to build your relationship upon. What kind of love will you be thinking of when you say your vows to cherish and honor one another? Will it be, "I promise to stay with you as long as you excite me and make me feel good"? Will it be, "I promise to behave in a manner that always pleases you"? Or will it be, "I promise to extend to you the grace, forgiveness, and love that God in Christ has given me"?

At this time, it is likely that your love for each other is energized by the ways your fiancé(e) thrills you. That's characteristic of romantic love. Understandably, your desire to fulfill each other romantically and sexually is in overdrive, and you are looking forward to your wedding night and your life together.

This section lays out the elements of love that God reveals in this chapter of His Word. You can have all the fireworks of romance without this type of love, but fireworks alone will not hold a marriage together. In fact, I read of a couple who were getting divorced and both agreed they had no problems in the sexual area. They had terrific sex but were getting divorced! Well, maybe they had great sensuality but not great intimacy. Intimacy can only grow in the fertile soil of God's kind of love. The following verses are what you will base your lives upon. They are the meaning of the vows you will be saying at the altar of your marriage. They are your launching pad to lifelong companionship and happiness as well as the passion you are looking forward to sharing.

When you have thoughtfully read and considered each verse, continue with the material on the following pages. We have separated the 16 elements of verses 4–8. Fill in the missing word(s) for each numbered space (1–16). Then on the lines below it, in your words, give your impression of the meaning of that particular element and how you will apply it in your relationship with your fiancé(e). How you will apply these characteristics of love to your relationship is a performance of sorts, but it is certainly different from the world's way, and it will yield the reward of a blessed life.

Before you start the following section, read 1 Corinthians chapter 13
(The NKJV was used for this exercise.)

Section 8 — Love

1 Corinthians 13:4–8 (NKJV)

Verse 4

(1) Love _____ long

Explain: _____
_____
_____

How I will apply it: _____
_____
_____
_____

(2) and is _____

Explain: _____
_____
_____

How I will apply it: _____
_____
_____
_____

(3) love does not _____

Explain: _____
_____
_____

How I will apply it: _____
_____
_____
_____

Section 8 *Love*

(4) love does not _____ itself

  Explain: _____
  _____
  _____
  _____

  How I will apply it: _____
  _____
  _____
  _____

(5) [love] is not _____ up

  Explain: _____
  _____
  _____
  _____

  How I will apply it: _____
  _____
  _____
  _____

Verse 5

(6) [love] does not behave _____

  Explain: _____
  _____
  _____
  _____

  How I will apply it: _____
  _____
  _____
  _____

Section 8   *Love*

(7)　[love] does not seek its _____

　　Explain: _____
　　_____
　　_____
　　_____

　　How I will apply it: _____
　　_____
　　_____
　　_____

(8)　[love] is not [easily] _____

　　Explain: _____
　　_____
　　_____
　　_____

　　How I will apply it: _____
　　_____
　　_____
　　_____

(9)　[love] thinks no _____

　　Explain: _____
　　_____
　　_____
　　_____

　　How I will apply it: _____
　　_____
　　_____
　　_____

Section 8 *Love*

Verse 6

(10) [love] does not rejoice in _____

Explain: _____

_____

_____

_____

How I will apply it: _____

_____

_____

_____

(11) but rejoices in _____

Explain: _____

_____

_____

_____

How I will apply it: _____

_____

_____

_____

Verse 7

(12) [love] _____ all things

Explain: _____

_____

_____

_____

How I will apply it: _____

_____

Section 8   *Love*

(13) [love] _____ all things

    Explain: _____

_____

_____

_____

    How I will apply it: _____

_____

_____

_____

_____

(14) [love] _____ all things,

    Explain: _____

_____

_____

_____

    How I will apply it: _____

_____

_____

_____

(15) [love] _____ all things.

    Explain: _____

_____

_____

_____

    How I will apply it: _____

_____

_____

_____

Section 8 *Love*

Verse 8

(16) Love never _____

Explain: _____

_____

_____

_____

_____

How I will apply it: _____

_____

_____

_____

_____

> **DO** → In the space below, write your definition of love. On the following page, write your version of what you think marriage vows should say. We are not suggesting that you write the actual vows you will say at your wedding. Some couples do compose their own vows, but often the pastor has vows the couple will repeat. This exercise is just for you to spend some time thinking about vows and about what constitutes worthy vows—ones you will honor and keep your whole lifetime.

(1) Your definition of love

_____

_____

_____

_____

_____

_____

_____

_____

Section 8 *Love*

(2) Your vow(s) to God and to your fiancé(e)

_____
_____
_____
_____
_____
_____
_____
_____
_____
_____
_____
_____
_____
_____
_____
_____
_____
_____
_____

Summing it up

I love pizza. I love my dog. I love skiing. I love my job. I love you.

Do all these "loves" mean the same thing? Even the words "I love you" can mean various shades and qualities of love, affection, devotion, commitment, exclusiveness, enjoyment, and endurance. The only similarity between a couple's intimacy and a pizza might be that both are hot and spicy! However, when you're looking into your beloved's eyes while saying your vows, we are confident you won't be thinking about pizza.

The point is this: You must have your definition of love clear in your own mind. You must be clear on what each of you means when you say "I love you." In fact, the next time you meet to discuss this section, ask your fiancé(e) to explain specifically what it means when he or she says the words "I love you."

Section 8 — Love

The Three Little Pigs

Along with all the fun and laughter and the companionship of loving and living together, you will experience such things as anger, conflicts, doubts, hurt feelings, disappointments, and misunderstandings. At some point down the road, you might question your choice of a partner. You might compare your spouse to other men or women. You may become disenchanted. His or her habits might bug you; they might loom up before you and block the view of the good traits. The routine of housework, jobs, paying bills, financial hardship, and other mundane things can easily become the background music of your relationship—the tune that always plays in the back of your mind and sets your general mood.

These things are some of the storms of life and marriage. When the storms hit, will your house stand? Will your love weather the storms?

The Three Little Pigs is a children's story that parallels Jesus' teaching (again, read Matthew 7:24). It has been a long time since I heard it, but as I recall, the first two pigs were lazy or foolish. They built their houses out of hay and sticks. When The Big Bad Wolf came, he huffed and puffed, and blew the houses down (and ate the pigs). The third pig took the time and effort to build his house with bricks, and although The Big Bad Wolf banged at the door to be let in, and then huffed and puffed, he could not blow the house down.

Who or what is The Big Bad Wolf? The wolf might be an interesting co-worker. If your spouse neglects you and takes you for granted, the guy or gal in the next cubicle will be ready and willing to give you all the attention you crave. What will you do?

The Big Bad Wolf might be the loss of respect and admiration you have for your husband as he makes one wrong decision after another. The wolf might be the fifty pounds your spouse puts on because keeping in shape is too much work. It sends the message that you are not worth the effort.

The Big Bad Wolf might be a debilitating illness or injury—constant physical pain that wears down your or your mate's body, your hearts, and your desire to get through another day. Such an illness takes up most of the attention and care in a relationship. If your mate has such an illness, will your love be there as the constant giver when little is being returned back to you? What kind of love will yours be?

Sticks or bricks? . . . What's your building material?

NOTES

FINANCES

The Bible has much to say about the blessings that come from trusting and obeying God. Throughout the Old Testament, there are stories of individuals, and Israel as a nation, being alternately blessed or cursed due do their adhering to or departing from God.

The foundation of America was in large part built on adherence to God and His Word. Because of that, we have reaped blessings beyond those of other nations. In America, there is abundant opportunity for achievement and lifestyle choice. Generally, there is nothing stopping anyone from pursuing an education, career, and lifestyle.

No matter what lifestyle we choose, we are to love God with our entire being–all our mind, soul, body, and strength (Deut. 6:4–5; Mark 12:28–30). Our entire being includes our money and what we do with it. The Bible says positive things about the wise use of money. Jesus even commended the unjust steward for his cunning and planning (Luke 16:1–8). The Bible also has much to say about the wrong use of money and the evil that comes from the love of money (Matt. 26:15). When we consider that some marriages break up over finances, we realize there is great importance in a godly attitude toward money and stewardship.

The purpose of this section is not to propose some standard of living as being either right or wrong. There is nothing virtuous about being rich (or about being poor for that matter). Jesus readily and equally embraced the rich and the poor. The purpose is to promote living for the Kingdom of God with *all* that we are, *all* that we have, and *all* that we do (Matt. 6:24–34). Anything other than that misses the high calling in Jesus Christ (Phil. 3:14). How this plays out in your lifestyle is between you, God, and your spouse.

Another purpose is to insure that within the parameters of living for the Kingdom of God, you are allowing yourself honestly held desires and realistic expectations. If your heart is set and fixed on His Kingdom, you will live for God no matter what your situation, lifestyle, and abilities. The parable of the talents makes this illustration. (See Matt. 25:14–30; Luke 19:12–27.)

Full disclosure is another reason for exploring your financial state and your plans in this area. With one couple we mentored, the man had undisclosed debt. The woman was distressed (to say the least) upon finding this out after they were married. Such a thing is a major blow to a spouse's ability to trust. Finances, careers, income, and spending—these are issues that we do not want to gloss over or take for granted. Neither should you.

Section 9 — Finances

Listed here are some of the many verses that speak of money, riches, and stewardship. After reading them, select a few from each column and summarize what they say.

1. Deut. 6:4–5
2. Deut. 8:7–14
3. 1 Chr. 29:12
4. Jer. 9:23–24
5. Prov. 8:10–11
6. Prov. 10:4
7. Prov. 13:22
8. Prov. 20:21
9. Prov. 22:7
10. Eccl. 5:10–11
11. Mal. 3:8–12
12. Matt. 6:19–21
13. Matt. 6:24–34
14. Matt. 19:23–26
15. Matt. 25:14–30
16. Matt. 26:14–15
17. Mark 10:17–27
18. Luke 8:14
19. Luke 12:15
20. Luke 16:1–15
21. Acts 4:32–37
22. Phil. 4:10–13, 19
23. 1 Tim. 6:6–10
24. 1 Tim. 6:17–19

Verse	Summary

Section 9 — Finances

FINANCIAL INVENTORY

Debt and credit

1. Have you completely revealed your financial situation to each other? (Ps. 51:6) (Yes/No) _____

2. Do you have debt? (Rom. 13:8) _____ How much? _____ What kind? _____
   _____

3. Do you have credit card debt? (Prov. 22:7) _____ How much? _____

4. How many credit cards do you have? _____

5. What is your credit rating? _____ Your fiancé(e)'s _____

6. a. Have you run a credit check on your fiancé(e)? _____ b. Does running a credit check seem distrustful to you? _____ c. Would you now consider running a credit check? _____

7. Is either of you advocating a prenuptial agreement? _____ If so, what are your thoughts and feelings about it? _____
   _____
   _____

8. Do you use credit cards? ☐ All the time ☐ Frequently ☐ Sometimes ☐ Never

9. Do you use credit cards to buy things you cannot afford? _____ Does your fiancé(e)? _____

10. Do you pay off credit cards promptly? _____ Does your fiancé(e)? _____

11. Do you use credit cards for convenience and have cash to back up your purchases? _____

12. Do you have student loans or other loans to pay off? _____ How much? _____

13. Do you have other financial obligations? _____ What are they?

    ☐ Mortgage   ☐ Car payment   ☐ Luxury items   ☐ Other _____
    ☐ Alimony   ☐ Child support ☐ Charities   _____

14. Will your fiancé(e)'s financial obligations become legally yours once you are married? _____

    If so, how do you feel about taking on your fiancé(e)'s debt or obligations? Do you feel:

    ☐ Supportive ☐ Understanding ☐ Imposed upon ☐ Frustrated ☐ Not applicable

    Comment _____
    _____
    _____

Section 9   *Finances*

15. If applicable, how will you feel about part of your spouse's (or your) paycheck going for alimony payments, child support, or other obligations incurred by your spouse?

    ☐ Supportive   ☐ Understanding   ☐ Imposed upon   ☐ Frustrated

    ☐ Jealous   ☐ Threatened   ☐ Resentful   ☐ Other _____

Managing money

16. Do you balance your checkbook regularly? _____   Does your fiancé(e)? _____

17. Do you overdraw your bank account(s)?   ☐ Often   ☐ Occasionally   ☐ Never

18. Are you aware of your fiancé(e)'s spending habits? _____   Are you uncertain? _____

19. Do you think your fiancé(e) spends too much money? (Matt. 6:19–21) _____

20. Is your fiancé(e) too tight with money? (Prov. 3:27–28) _____

21. Do you pay bills on time? _____ Does your fiancé(e)? _____

22. Will you have separate bank accounts? _____ If so, why _____
    _____

23. Who will oversee the finances, pay bills, balance the books, etc.? _____

24. Since you are not yet married, is it your place to be concerned about, or to voice concern about, your fiancé(e)'s income or spending habits? _____

25. Do you expect your fiancé(e)'s financial habits to change once you are married? _____

26. Characterize your spending habits _____
    _____
    _____

27. Characterize your fiancé(e)'s spending habits _____
    _____
    _____

28. Comment on your fiancé(e)'s attitude about finances and lifestyle. (See Eccl. 5:11; Matt. 25:14–30.)
    _____
    _____
    _____
    _____

Section 9　　　　　　　　　　　　　　　　　　　　　　*Finances*

Career and Income

29. Which of you makes the higher income? _____ How much higher? _____

30. If the woman makes more money than the man, is that a problem? _____

31. (Man) Is it uncomfortable for you if your fiancée makes more than you do? _____

32. (Woman) Are you uncomfortable if he doesn't make as much or more than you do? _____

33. (Woman) If you make more income, does this diminish your respect for your fiancé? _____

34. Are you satisfied with your income? _____ With your fiancé(e)'s income? _____

35. Are you where you want to be with your career and your finances? _____

36. Will you still be happy if you: Don't reach your career goals? _____ Have to settle for a lot less income? _____ Have to take a job that is less than what you want or think you are worth? _____

Investing

37. Have you had financial counseling? _____ If not, are you interested in getting counseling? _____

38. Do you put money aside regularly into a savings account? _____

39. Briefly, describe your investment strategy. _____
_____
_____

40. What are your thoughts on tithing or other support of a church or ministry? _____
_____
_____

41. Are you currently giving financially to a ministry? _____ Describe _____
_____
_____

Life Insurance

42. Do you have life insurance? _____ If not, will you buy life insurance when you marry? _____

43. Is life insurance a viable way of protecting your family? Comment _____
_____
_____

Section 9　　　　　　　　　　　　　　　　　　　Finances

Budget worksheet

44. For the purpose of this budget worksheet, assume you are married and have combined your households and finances.

Net monthly income of husband　$ _____　　Net monthly income of wife $ _____

Monthly income other sources　$ _____　　Total net monthly income　$ _____

Estimated joint tax liability yearly　$ _____

Combined Monthly Expenses	Amount (approx.)
Tithes, offerings, support of ministries	$
Savings	
Investments	
Mortgage or rent on personal residence	
Other mortgages	
Child support – alimony payments	
Monthly debt – credit card payments	
Student loans – schooling	
Automobile payments	
Auto maintenance/purchase fund	
Gasoline	
Auto Insurance	
Home Insurance	
Health Insurance	
Life Insurance	
Medical/dental care	
Utilities (gas, water, electric, cable, trash)	
Home phone	
Cell phones	
Internet providers	
Groceries/household supplies	
Eating out	
Recreation & Entertainment	
Personal (hair salon, cosmetics, clothes, etc.)	
Other monthly expenses	
COMBINED NET MONTHLY INCOME	
TOTAL COMBINED MONTHLY EXPENSES	
DIFFERENCE + or –	

Section 9   *Finances*

Any other comments or concerns about finances?

_____
_____
_____
_____
_____
_____
_____
_____
_____
_____
_____
_____

Summing it up

This section only skims the surface of finances. There are many resources for managing family finances including financial planners, software, books, Web sites, seminars, and ministries. We highly recommend taking a financial planning and preparation course or setting up individual meetings with a financial counselor. Perhaps your church sponsors financial planning courses and seminars. If it does not, there are some well-established organizations offering them. Two popular organizations are listed below.

Crown Financial Ministries   Financial Peace University
http://www.crown.org   http://www.daveramsey.com

Section 9 — Finances

NOTES

SEX

Except for breathing, drinking, and eating, nothing is as intense as our romantic and sexual expression of love. Sexual love is natural, and generally, we go for it with gusto. But, we also know that nothing else seemingly causes more trouble and suffering—personally and for society. As with other aspects of relationship, sexuality is vulnerable to such things as the following: poor communication, disagreement, differing expectations, unawareness, sin, habits, and distorted views from experiences, upbringing, and religious indoctrination.

A couple of things need to be said up front.

First, these matters are deeply personal; it is a delicate thing to invite a third party (your mentors) into a discussion about your sexuality. Thus, we want to strike a balance. We want to respect your privacy and godly propriety, yet we also realize that this area should not be skipped over because of embarrassment, fear, or taking it for granted that everything is okay.

Second, the Bible does not address specifically and explicitly every area of sexuality, and we want to avoid twisting Scripture in an attempt to do so. Aside from what can be gleaned from the Song of Solomon, Scripture doesn't delve into such things as techniques, performance, frequency, etc. Nevertheless, it does provide abundant instruction and exhortation on loving and respecting your spouse and about what constitutes love and respect. All intimate issues come under the umbrella of godly love and respectful care for your spouse. In addition to the Song of Solomon, guidance can be gleaned from other Scriptures such as: Genesis 2:23–25; Proverbs 5:15–20; 1 Corinthians 7:1–5; Philemon 4:8 and Hebrews 13:4.

Third, many of you are virgins. For you, the discovery and enjoyment of sex are before you. You do not need to have—you are not expected to have—answers for some of these questions. Some questions will not apply to you because they are directed to those who have been previously married or who have been sexually active. For some, this is your second or more marriage. Others have been promiscuous before coming to Christ, and some have suffered sexual abuse and exploitation. Bear with us as we attempt to cover the bases for a variety of situations.

You might feel some questions are too explicit and invasive, and you may choose not to share your thoughts and feelings with your mentors. That is completely acceptable. Just realize that many of the questions address common and problematic issues. The important thing is that you discuss sex (at least in a general way) with your fiancé(e) and are in agreement with your views. Also, discuss your views with each other before meeting with your mentors. This will help you to bond and to avoid surprises and embarrassment during the meeting.

Finally, your mentoring couple should be sensitive to your privacy and to what is appropriate while also seeking to address fears, expectations, inexperience, or other concerns. Remember that they are human too. They have their own issues, struggles, successes, and failures. We expect they are (they should be) a mature couple who have a deep love for God and for each other. They should relate to you with candor and humility in a way that puts you at ease. This area, like your relationship to God, is no place for legalistic treatment.

Section 10   Sex

SEX SURVEY

1. Check any items that you think apply (will apply) to your attitudes about sex.

   ☐ It's fun, enjoyable, and euphoric.   ☐ It's an inconvenience.
   ☐ It's God's gift and blessing.   ☐ I *can* live without it.
   ☐ It's to be tolerated.   ☐ I *can't* live without it.
   ☐ I'm looking forward to it.   ☐ It's a wife's (or husband's) duty.
   ☐ I'm apprehensive about our wedding night.   ☐ I'm uninterested in it.
   ☐ I have some apprehensions about sex.   ☐ I'm unknowledgeable about it.
   ☐ I'm concerned about rejection.   ☐ It's mainly for childbearing.
   ☐ I'm concerned about my performance.   ☐ I want to learn more about technique.
   ☐ I'm concerned about my spouse's performance. ☐ My (or my spouse's) past might affect our sexual oneness.

Do the following inventory on a scale of 1 – 5 (5 being best, most, most agreeable, etc.).
Circle the number that represents your response.

Note: Allow these questions to spark amplification and clarification of your views

	Disagree ←		Agree →		
2. I am comfortable discussing these matters with my fiancé(e).	1	2	3	4	5
3. We have discussed our sexual desires and expectations sufficiently.	1	2	3	4	5
4. I know what my fiancé(e) views, desires, and needs are.	1	2	3	4	5
5. My fiancé(e) places too much importance and emphasis on sex.	1	2	3	4	5
6. My fiancé(e) doesn't place enough importance and emphasis on sex.	1	2	3	4	5
7. We have crossed the boundaries we set for our engagement.	1	2	3	4	5
8. Sex is God's idea; He wants married couples to enjoy it.	1	2	3	4	5
9. Sin has marred our (mankind's) sexual nature.	1	2	3	4	5
10. When married, I want to be provocative, alluring, seductive, exciting.	1	2	3	4	5
11. I would like my spouse to be provocative, alluring, and seductive.	1	2	3	4	5
12. In marriage, anything is okay.	1	2	3	4	5
13. In marriage, there is no such thing as sexual abuse.	1	2	3	4	5
14. Withholding sex can be a desire to control, manipulate, or punish.	1	2	3	4	5

Section 10 — Sex

	Disagree → Agree
15. Demanding sex can be a desire to control, manipulate, or punish.	1 2 3 4 5
16. Sexual intimacy should satisfy emotional and relational needs and well-being as well as the purely physical needs and drives.	1 2 3 4 5
17. Within marriage, there could be such a thing as unwholesome sex.	1 2 3 4 5
18. Sex is an expression of love, care, commitment, and consideration for each other, more so than physical passion or physical appetite.	1 2 3 4 5
19. Sex is an urge that can't be controlled.	1 2 3 4 5
20. Sex will be fun.	1 2 3 4 5
21. Some fantasies are perfectly okay.	1 2 3 4 5
22. Some types of erotic material (movies, pictures, etc.) are okay.	1 2 3 4 5
23. I'm concerned my mate won't be very pleased with my body.	1 2 3 4 5
24. My goal in sex will be to please my mate rather than myself.	1 2 3 4 5
25. Lovemaking is an art and a skill to be learned and improved upon. It takes patience, time, and gentle acceptance of each other.	1 2 3 4 5
26. Sex is mainly a guy thing. It's more for men than it is for women.	1 2 3 4 5
27. Men get more enjoyment out of sex than women do.	1 2 3 4 5
28. I am rather unknowledgeable about technique—the art of lovemaking	1 2 3 4 5
29. I would like some help via book referrals or private talks with a discreet, same-gender mentor.	1 2 3 4 5
30. Men typically have stronger sex drives than women.	1 2 3 4 5
31. We should abstain from intercourse during menstrual cycles.	1 2 3 4 5
32. We agree about sexual technique, positions, activities, etc.	1 2 3 4 5
33. Only men have orgasms.	1 2 3 4 5
34. Orgasms are not important for women to have.	1 2 3 4 5
35. Women can experience orgasms of greater intensity and duration than men.	1 2 3 4 5
36. Women should not initiate sex.	1 2 3 4 5
37. Men, in general, would like their wife to initiate sex often.	1 2 3 4 5

Section 10 — Sex

	Disagree ←			→ Agree	
38. I wish some things about my body were different.	1	2	3	4	5
39. The "missionary" position is the only appropriate way to have sex.	1	2	3	4	5
40. Sex is (it will be) a great stress reliever.	1	2	3	4	5
41. Sex will be a continual bonding and strengthening of our union.	1	2	3	4	5
42. Lust (fantasizing an affair) is not the same as actual adultery.	1	2	3	4	5
43. Sex is for (or primarily for):					
Having children	1	2	3	4	5
Recreation – about having fun and physical pleasure	1	2	3	4	5
Relationship – about maintaining and improving relationship	1	2	3	4	5
Giving the other person his or her "fix"	1	2	3	4	5
A pressure relief valve to keep passions under control	1	2	3	4	5
Keeping a man (or woman) at home	1	2	3	4	5
Controlling your mate	1	2	3	4	5
44. Men are much more stimulated by visual sensation than women are.	1	2	3	4	5
45. There are things about my mate's body (looks) I wish were different.	1	2	3	4	5
46. Women are more stimulated by "setting the mood"— loving, affectionate words, candlelight, and thoughtful actions.	1	2	3	4	5
47. Godliness and wholesomeness should characterize sexual intimacy.	1	2	3	4	5

By the way . . .

Man: Do you realize that her strong desire for hugs and physical closeness is likely *not* a restrained desire for wild, passionate sex that you might interpret it to be? Do you realize that, when you are finally married, she might not magically morph into the voracious sexual creature you think she is and that you want and expect her to be—the creature she seems to be broadcasting with all her premarital touching and hugging?

Woman: Do you truly understand and accept that the male sex drive is God-made, that it is not (necessarily) his unredeemed flesh or animalistic urges he must learn to deny? God designed his desire for sex—just as He designed your desire for hugs and snuggling. Consider this: When you are married, if your husband gives you hugs with the same enthusiasm that you give him sex, would you be satisfied?

Section 10 — Sex

SEXUALITY AND PROBLEMATIC ISSUES

In the following section, you are asked to comment on various issues, but, again, to do so might be invasive. You need not answer these questions to your mentoring couple if you feel they violate your boundaries.

Having said that, you are in the process of establishing the most intimate and self-exposing relationship a person can have. Being physically naked with your spouse is one thing; but it is another thing to be emotionally and mentally naked—revealing the deepest kept secrets—your deepest hopes, passions, insecurities, fears, shame, sins, and wounds. Sometimes it's a lot safer to give your body than to give your heart. Self-preservation is our nature; we are apt to hold back anything that would threaten our sense of security and our sense of being in control. Yet, you are establishing the most intimate relationship possible—one you will be in for a half century or longer. A little discomfort now can save you a lot of distress in the future.

Write your comments to the following questions or statements. If you do not comment on these issues to your mentors, you should at least be clear in your own mind about these things and then be appropriately transparent with your soon-to-be spouse.

1. Describe your views on sex and sexuality. _____
   _____
   _____
   _____

2. Do you have any fears or hang-ups about sexual relationship or performance? _____ If so, have you discussed these things with your fiancé(e)? _____

   Explain _____
   _____
   _____

3. Are there experiences or relationships that might affect your upcoming sexual relations? _____

   If yes, explain _____
   _____
   _____

4. Have you ever had a sexually transmitted disease(s) of any kind? (Yes/No) _____ Have you ever been tested for any type of STD? _____ Are you willing to be tested? _____

5. Do you have a high, moderate, or low desire for sex? _____

6. How often do you think you would like to have sex? _____ times per (circle) Day Week Month

7. Do you fantasize about previous relationships or others?   ☐ Often   ☐ Sometimes   ☐ Never

Section 10 — Sex

8. Are you using pornography, Internet porn, or videos rated for sexual content? (Yes/No) _____

9. Have you in the past used or been addicted to pornographic material? (Yes/No) _____

10. What is your belief about pornography; what constitutes pornography? _____
    _____
    _____

11. What is your belief about R and PG13 movies rated for sexual content? _____
    _____
    _____

12. Are you and your fiancé(e) in agreement about movies and videos? _____

13. Have you talked openly and comfortably about your sexual needs, desires, and hopes? _____

14. Is a strong sex drive a sign of lack of spirituality or a lack of self-control? _____

15. Have you been honest with your fiancé(e) about past sexual involvements? _____

16. a. Have you read any books or listened to audio/video messages about sex within marriage? _____

    b. If so, which resources? _____
    _____
    _____

17. a. Do you have any concerns about your soon-to-be sexual relationship, the honeymoon, etc.? _____

    b. If so, what are those concerns?

    ☐ Inadequacy   ☐ Obsessive desire for sex
    ☐ Rejection   ☐ Poor performance on your or your mate's part
    ☐ Your appearance   ☐ Lack of knowledge
    ☐ Failure to satisfy your mate ☐ Other _____
    ☐ Pain or discomfort   ☐ _____

18. a. If your spouse were to give someone else the eye (a second look), how would that make you feel?
    _____
    _____
    _____

    b. How would you respond? _____
    _____
    _____

Section 10 — Sex

19. Is it ever OK to say "no," or must one always accommodate his/her spouse? Comment
    _____
    _____

20. What sexual acts, positions, etc., do you (will you) find repugnant? _____
    _____
    _____
    _____

21. Comment on any sexual violations you have experienced. _____
    _____
    _____
    _____

22. Have you been promiscuous? _____   If so, how might this affect your relationship now?
    _____
    _____
    _____

23. Is sex outside of marriage a sin? Is the injunction to abstain from sex outside of marriage a religious rule . . . a social custom . . . a personal choice? Comment _____
    _____
    _____

24. With 10 being most, circle how important sex is to you.   1 2 3 4 5 6 7 8 9 10

25. In your own opinion, what would be perverted, sinful sex? _____
    _____

26. Have you ever been involved in homosexual/lesbian experiences, affairs, or lifestyles? _____ Or have you had secret urges to do so, or that you struggle against, that you haven't acted upon? _____

    If so, before doing this section, have you already shared these things with your fiancé(e)? _____

27. Any other comments about sexuality? _____
    _____

Section 10 — Sex

Summarizing sexual problems

Sexual problems may be rooted in various causes, such as the following:

a. Problems that emanate from lack of knowledge and experience

b. Problems that emanate from physical/hormonal/medical conditions

c. Problems that emanate from habits and/or sin

- Pornography, lust (wandering eyes), same sex attraction
- Idolatry (idolizing sex or the worship of the body – physical beauty)

d. Problems that emanate from experiences

- Childhood abuse
- Promiscuity
- Former marriage(s) or relationship(s)

e. Problems that emanate from emotional disconnects

- Guilt
- Fear
- Shame
- Distancing, self-protection
- Disagreements, arguments, fights, unresolved conflicts

f. Problems that emanate from differing views about sex or unrealistic expectations

g. Problems that emanate from selfishness, self-seeking, and self-centered gratification

- Sexploitation – Sexual abuse
- Relationship based on sexual performance
- Using sex as manipulation
- Using sex as a means to conquer–to achieve a sense of power, self-esteem.
- Using sex as a cover for other issues (lack of relational intimacy, bonding, anger, cruelty, abuse, inadequacy, low self-worth)

Some facts about common misconceptions

- Marriage will not cure or solve sinful (aberrant) sexual problems.
- Pornography is not an issue of just needing a mate. Marriage does not cure it.
- If someone has a sexual addiction, he or she will continue with it even when married.
- Marriage is not the solution for sexual addictions or sexual obsession. (Perhaps a better way to say it is that marriage it is not the "cure" for sexual addictions or sexual obsession.)[1]

---

[1] According to 1 Cor. 7:9, marriage is the solution for those who cannot contain their sexual passions. However, Paul was likely considering normal sex drives rather than lust that manifests in pornography and other expressions of sexual addiction and obsession. Witness the fact that so many married people are struggling with deeply entrenched sexual sin. If marriage is the cure, they would not be involved with such sins.

Section 10 — Sex

THE WEDDING NIGHT, HONEYMOON, AND BEYOND

You have spent the last months (or years) preparing for this day. A great amount of time and mental and emotional investment has been put into this moment. The stress and pressure have been building slowly like a wave. Then comes the moment of catching and riding the wave—your wedding day is here. No matter whether it is a large, complex ceremony or a small and simple one, you will to some degree experience the intensity of the moment and everything that has led up to it.

Some couples handle these things in stride and are not too stressed on their wedding day. Others can be so tightly wound, that it's all they can do to remember their names and say their vows! In this moment, all the attention is on you, and your focus is on performance, you want it to happen perfectly. When the ceremony is over, and the reception is ending, and just when you think you can relax, another ceremony looms before you: the wedding night—another giant performance!

A lot of expectation can be built into the wedding night. It's supposed to be the most romantic moment of your lives up until now. You want your wedding to be "magical" and you want your wedding night to be just as magical. Some couples stay at a nearby hotel on their wedding night before zooming off on their honeymoon, and some endure a long flight to their honeymoon destination on their first night. Unless you are two very hardy souls with the physical endurance of Olympic athletes, don't burden yourselves with unrealistic expectations for your wedding night. If you both have the strength and the emotional wherewithal, and your hormones are in supercharged mode—overriding every other bodily message—you may experience a very enjoyable first night. Many do and many do not. If you are just too tired, nervous, wound up, or in la la land, don't let it bother you, and don't be disappointed with yourself or your spouse. Couples have told us they were both too exhausted and that they chose to sleep their first night. (There's always the day after, you know!)

Other than the stress of the ceremony and physical and emotional exhaustion, there are practical matters concerning the wedding night—notably, pain or discomfort for the virgin woman. Therefore, speaking to you guys, be understanding and gentle. Your hormonal horses are bursting to get out of the starting gate, but be considerate of your new bride. Doing so will pay great dividends to you once her internal parts have acclimated.

Some things to be aware of and to make allowances for are:

- Inexperience
- Pain or discomfort
- Lubricants
- Birth control

- Being relaxed with each other
- Setting the mood
- Too physical – not enough relational connection
- Not as thrilling as expected

Beyond your honeymoon

Beyond your honeymoon, the first weeks, months, and year(s) of your marriage will be a time of great adjustment. Your sexuality will be a time of learning, discovery, and experimenting. Some couples experience pressure and frustration from high expectations. The pressure to have incredible sex (orgasms, for example) can make the experience all the more difficult. In order to have an enjoyable sexual experience, women need a safe, secure, private environment—one that is free of relational conflict and free of expectation or performance pressures. What women need foremost is trust and security in their husband's love and care. The consensus among women is that they want and need relationship much more on a nonsexual level before they are able to enjoy sex and give themselves to their husbands with abandon.

NOTES

Appendix

Congratulations

You have completed an intensive course that was full of probing questions about almost every area of your life and your relationship. We believe it is important to turn over every stone possible in the preparation of two people becoming one. Every couple we know who have used this book has been amazed at how much they learn about themselves and about each other and about how much they didn't know to ask each other. If such is the case with you, we think you will agree that your relationship has been helped and improved and that, having used this workbook, you are better prepared for marriage and for the road ahead. That is our goal and hope.

We also hope you have had a very enjoyable time using this material to prepare for your marriage. If you have used this book with a mentoring couple, we hope that your experience with them has been encouraging, uplifting, and beneficial. Perhaps you have established a friendship with them that will last a lifetime.

If you have any comments or questions about the workbook, the course, the mentoring experience, or about your relationship, please contact us. We would enjoy and appreciate hearing from you. This book is a work in progress, and we thoughtfully and prayerfully consider comments and suggestions we receive.

God bless you in your marriage. Live in His grace.

Mike & Jewel Williamson

Building Your Marriage Upon the Rock

THE IN-DEPTH PREMARITAL WORKBOOK WITH
THE BIBLE AS YOUR AUTHORITY AND GUIDE

ISBN 978-0-9794715-1-3

Genesis224 is the marriage and premarital ministry of Mike & Jewel Williamson

To order this workbook, or for information on premarital mentoring and marriage relationships, visit our Websites:

www.premaritalworkbook.com
www.genesis224.com

Appendix

Appendix

WEDDING STATISTICS [1]

ENGAGEMENT STATISTICS

- The average American engagement is 16 months.
- During the engagement period, couples buy $4 billion in furniture, $3 billion in house wares, $400 million in tableware
- Every year an average of 2.4 million weddings are performed in the U.S.
- The Wedding Industry is a 50 billion dollar a year industry
- One third of engaged couples retain a wedding consultant
- An average honeymoon vacation is one week
- Bridesmaids' gowns are generally purchased 3–4 months in advance of the event
- Most brides (30%) plan their weddings for 7 to 12 months

COST STATISTICS

- $22,000 is the average amount spent on a traditional American wedding
- A total of $72 billion is spent on weddings annually in the U.S.
- $19 billion is spent buying presents at wedding gift registries
- The average amount spent on a bridal gown is $800
- The average ring costs $2,000

WEDDING COSTS BY CATEGORY (% cost)

- Reception 28.3%
- Consultant 15.0% (if hired)
- Wedding rings 11.5%
- Photography/Video 6.6%
- Bridal gown 6.1%
- Music 5.2%
- Flowers 4.6%
- Bridal attendants' apparel 4.5%
- Rehearsal dinner 4.2%
- Invitations 2.8%
- Men's formal wear 3.2%
- Attendants' gifts 2.1%
- Mother of the bride apparel 1.7%
- Bride's veil 1.6%
- Clergy and ceremony fees 1.2%
- Limousine 0.9%

OTHER WEDDING STATISTICS

- 80% of traditional weddings are performed in churches or synagogues.
- There is a 43% chance of a marriage ending in divorce.
- Percentage of couples living together before marriage: 64%
- 30% of receptions are held in churches; 20% in hotels; 20% in country clubs; and 10% each in fraternal halls, private homes, and other locations.
- More than 4.2 million unmarried couples live together.

HONEYMOON STATISTICS

- Couples spend an average of $4,000 on their honeymoon. That's three times as much as the average U.S. adult spends on a vacation.
- The length of an average honeymoon is seven days.
- The Honeymoon Industry is a 12 billion dollar a year industry.

---

[1] Based on a 2006 survey. The online source is no longer available.

Appendix

MYTHS ABOUT COHABITATION

> *"The truth is that wherever a man lies with a woman, there, whether they like it or not, a transcendental relation is setup between them which must be eternally enjoyed or eternally endured."* --C. S. Lewis, Screwtape Letters

There are a number of reasons given today for living together, most of which are based on current popular myths. Several (fourteen) of the most common myths of the day are:

Myth # 1:

Everybody's doing it!

First, everybody is *not* "doing it." Statistics show that of the college-age people, 65 to 80 percent are sexually active and some of those are living together (Marco 1997). Johnson (1996) estimates 30 to 40 percent of college students cohabit during their time at college. Although this is a large number, this also indicates that somewhere between 20 and 35 percent are not sexually active and somewhere around 60 to 70 percent of students do not cohabit. Therefore, to say "everybody's doing it," is a myth and does not hold up as a valid justification for cohabiting.

Second, a 1994 poll by ICR Survey Research Group for USA Weekend asked more than 1,200 teens and adults what they thought of "several high profile athletes (who) are saying in public that they have abstained from sex before marriage and are telling teens to do the same." Seventy-two percent of the 12- to 17-year-olds and 78 percent of the adults said that they agree with the pro-abstinence message. Moreover, 44 percent of those under the age of 18 said, "today's teenagers hear too little about saying no to sex." (Tom McNichol, "Sex Can Wait," USA Weekend, March 25-227, 1994, pp. 4–6.)

Third, in a recent statement by the Catholic Bishops of Pennsylvania they said, "just because everyone does something doesn't make it right or any less serious. A couple's choice to live together is not simply made in isolation. It affects everyone in relationship with these two people —parents, brothers, sisters, friends, and even other members of the parish. A cohabiting couple implicitly communicates that there is nothing wrong with breaking God's law. This can be especially misleading to young children—nieces, nephews, and children of friends—who are impressionable and whose moral reasoning is immature."

Myth # 2:

Economically it's worth it to live together.

First, it is cheaper for two to live together. However, whatever monetary or other savings are realized from making the choice to living together, [there] is also the price at which one will compromise, lose, or sell out one's moral standards, virginity, and purity.

Second, economical advantages don't in themselves determine whether something is morally right or wrong.

Third, the majority of cohabitants do eventually break up and economics are obviously not an overwhelming impediment then, so why allow it to become a controlling factor from the start. The moral questions ought to be "What is my virginity worth?" and "Will I save myself for my lifelong spouse?" Kevin Leman in Smart Kids, Stupid Choices says, "It's kind of like giving someone a million dollars and later finding out you gave it to the wrong person, but now he's

Appendix

gone and so is your money—gone for good. You don't have it anymore. And the person who should have had it will now never get it."

A 2005 study, published in the Journal of Marriage and the Family (Smock) looked at the relationship between economic uncertainty and relationship conflict. Researchers interviewed 115 young adults in the vicinity of Toledo, Ohio, who were cohabiting or had recently cohabited, and found that among cohabiters financial uncertainty and a lack of money were associated with relationship conflict and the lack of a "sense of a stable future," thus inhibiting the decision to marry.

In a recent statement by the Catholic Bishops of Pennsylvania, they said, sure, you might save the price of monthly rent, but you're sacrificing something more valuable. Engagement is more than just time to plan the party. It is a time for deeper discussion and thorough reflection, which are best carried out in a detached way. Couples who are living together do not have the luxury of such detachment. So, whatever expenses you save, you'll likely pay more in the end.

Dr. Joyce Brothers said it well in an article on cohabitation: "short-term savings are less important than investing in a lifetime relationship."

A study published in the Journal of Marriage and Family (Wilmoth 2002) of 9,137 retired individuals looks at the relationship between marital status and wealth. It found that cohabiters who never marry have 78 percent less wealth than the continuously married, and cohabiters who have been divorced or widowed once have 68 percent less wealth. Cohabiters who have been divorced or widowed twice are not significantly different from the continuously married group.

Myth # 3:

Living together before marriage increases your chances of having a happy marriage later.

You "test drive a car" before you buy it, so why not do the same with your lifelong relationships. Another one that is heard often is, "you try on a pair of shoes to see if they fit before you buy them, why not your spouse." Someone has said, when you test drive a car you don't pack your personal luggage in the trunk or when you try on a pair of new shoes you don't want everyone else's foot odor and fungus already in them. You can throw away shoes without hurting anyone, but you can't throw away a person without hurting them and possibly others. The great paradox is that research indicates just the opposite of this conventional 'wisdom'. Numerous studies (see "Reasons" below) have shown that couples who have lived together before marriage are more likely to disagree on things like recreation, household chores and finances and are more likely to seek counseling than couples who do not cohabit.

Commentator Andrew Greeley (1991) states, "There is no support for the folk wisdom that premarital sex of one variety or another is a preparation for marital happiness."

A study (Kamp Duch 2003) of 306 married individuals between the ages of 19 and 40 who had married between 1981 and 1997 and 1,119 married individuals who were married between 1964 and 1980, looked at the relationship between marital quality and conflict and cohabiting for cohabiters of two different age cohorts. It found that respondents married between 1981 and 1997 as well as for those married between 1964 and 1980, those who cohabited before marriage reported less marital happiness and greater marital conflict than those who did not cohabit.

Appendix

Myth # 4:

Doing it won't hurt anyone.

Marco (1997) lists several statistics for college age people, including the facts that 63 percent of all STDs happen to people less than 25 and more than 20 percent of all persons with AIDS are college age. Many people are permanently hurt, either emotionally or physically, or both. Even those not directly involved such as your friends and parents may get hurt. Sin is like throwing a pebble in a pond, it involves only the pebble and the water, but it sends ripples across the entire pond. Sin is never solitary. One's philosophy of life is like the controlling formula of a spreadsheet where a change of one cell affects the entire outcome at the end. Man sometimes lives as though one single behavior or event is an isolated cell that doesn't affect another; but it does. When one part is changed, it changes the whole of it.

Myth # 5:

It's nobody's business.

It is said that living together has much in common with marriage except for the legal imposition of the church and state. However, birth, health, and disease issues are a consequence of cohabiting, and they do very much become the responsibility and expense of society. The church is a vital part of society and as such, has the responsibility to uphold that which is the best for society. If the couple wants to be married in the church, then it does become church business.

The church itself also has the responsibility to uphold scriptural standards of purity, which is its business. We are admonished in Scripture and have the responsibility to speak the truth in love (Eph. 4:15). Also, churches help launch and keep lasting marriages. Frequent church attendees have lower divorce rates because they are exposed to teaching and instruction on marital success and because the church body lends support and accountability to couples (Mattox 1997).

"The Church is particularly concerned about cohabitation because the practice is so common today and because, in the long run, it is causing great unhappiness for families in the Church. This is true, above all, because—although society may approve of the practice—cohabitation simply cannot be squared with God's plan for marriage. This may be why most couples who live together before marriage find married life difficult to sustain for very long. The Church does not invent laws. It passes on and interprets what God has revealed through the ages. No one in the Church has the right to change what Jesus has taught. To do so would be to deprive people of saving truths that were meant for all time. Our Christian faith teaches that a sexual relationship belongs only in marriage. Sex outside of marriage shows disrespect for the institution of marriage, the sacredness of sex, and human dignity" (Bishops of Pennsylvania).

Myth # 6:

It's all right because we're really in love!

First, love can never be a reason for premarital sex; rather, it is one of the greatest reasons to avoid premarital sex (Martin & Myers 1996). True love would never seek the spiritual downfall of another (Rom. 13:10). The Scripture says that love is patient and kind; it does not seek to please itself, nor does it delight in evil, but is always hopeful (1 Cor. 13). Therefore, true love is patient in waiting for the proper time for sex. It is kind to future spouses by not pre-harming marital intimacy. True love would be unselfish in placing God's will and the needs of others above self. It would not delight in the evil of disobedience, nor would it force another to disobey God (Martin & Myers 1996).

Appendix

Second, the 'feelings of love' are tricky. Jim Long in Campus Life (February 1986) states, "Love can fool you. Your feelings can trick you. The line between love and infatuation is thin. And frankly, sex confuses everything. To be physically involved clouds the issue. It makes you feel closer than you really are. It makes you feel as if you are actually in love. Maybe so. Maybe not."

Third, living together is a form of prostitution and love. Dunagan (1993), for example, explains the Greek word rendered 'fornication' is 'porneia', which also means prostitution, and 'porne' was the word for prostitute. God chose these words to describe and label any sexual activity outside of marriage. (1 Cor. 7:9; Matt. 19:9). Fornication is essentially the love that is bought or sold, which is not love at all. The person with whom such 'love' (lust) is gratified is not really considered a person at all, but a thing. He or she is a mere instrument through which the demands of lust and passion are satisfied. God is letting us know that to call such 'love' is false.

Myth # 7:

But we're going to be married anyway.

This is presumptuous, naive, and wishful thinking. There is often one person in the relationship who doesn't think in terms of a permanent, lifelong relationship. The lingering question is "If one gives in to moral temptation before marriage, what's going to be different and prevent them from repeating the behavior once the honeymoon is over?"

Myth # 8:

The Bible doesn't teach that a civil or religious ceremony must be performed for marriage to be valid in God's eye, so why have one?

The institution of marriage was first created and ordained of God (Gen. 2) and all marriages are still blessings ordained by Him in order that two may become one. It is evident that in biblical times there was a contractual agreement, perhaps verbal, signifying marriage. The parables of "The Wedding Garment" (Matt. 22:11–14) and "The Ten Virgins" (Matt. 25:1–13) indicate that marriage took place at a given time and place. The Scripture says, "Give to Caesar what is Caesar's and to God what is God's" (Matt. 22:21; Mark 12:17 & Luke 20:25). The government (the 'Caesar' of our day) requires that we must have a marriage license in order to be legally recognized. Since a marriage ceremony is a civil requirement, we are obligated as law-abiding citizens and Christians to observe it.

Myth # 9:

It'll enhance my self-esteem and inner security.

Marco (1997) provides a quote that he believes best sums up what the studies show: "I slept with many, many people trying to find love, to find self-worth. And the more people I slept with the less self-worth I had." It makes sense he says, when you give yourself as "pieces" to a lot of people, you are no longer whole, and as a consequence, may actually feel less self-worth and inner security—because part(s) of you is (are) missing.

Myth # 10:

The Bible is silent on the subject.

A common myth heard often is that there is nothing in the Bible condemning a couple for having physical relations before marriage. 1 Corinthians 7:2 says, "but, because of fornication, let each man have his own wife, and let each woman have her own husband." Dunagan (1993) explains, 'Fornication' is unlawful sexual activity of any kind. In this verse, Paul places the marriage

Appendix

relationship in contrast to fornication. Fornication can be avoided when you have your own spouse. Therefore, 'fornication—unlawful sexual activity' exists in a relationship in which a man and woman are physically intimate, and yet not married. And the Bible is very clear regarding the consequences of fornication (1 Cor. 6:9; Gal. 5:19–21; Rev. 21:8; Heb.13:4). In addition, Paul informs those that don't have the self-control to live the single life, to marry. (1 Cor. 7:9).

Myth # 11:

The marriage license is only a piece of paper, and it doesn't automatically make two people committed to each other.

"It won't make me love you more." "We are already committed to each other, we don't need a piece of paper to prove it." Dunagan (1993) presents the other side of the argument: "If there's no difference in your relationship, what's wrong with adding one more symbol to your total commitment?" Evidently, marriage consists of more than just a piece of paper. After all, Dunagan says, (makes the following questions and statements:)

> Who raises strong objections over *just a piece of paper*?
>
> Who has ever objected to buying a ring (or anything nice) just to prove their love?
>
> We're committed to each other, we love each other, we don't need to sleep together to prove that we love each other.
>
> I love you (and I am) really committed to you, but not for a lifetime.
>
> I love you, but not enough to want you to be my wife.
>
> I love you, but not enough to want to wear your last name.
>
> I love you, but not enough to vow such love before God, family and friends.
>
> I love you, but not enough to enter a relationship that brings you honor, respect, and preserves your dignity.

Myth # 12:

Cohabitation, marriage, and divorce are, can be, or should be, just another lifestyle choice, a purely personal relationship created by and for the couple.

This is the "most powerful and dangerous myth," according to Waite and Gallagher (2000:6) because it goes to the heart of the issue. There is an increasing tendency today to view marriage not as objective fact, but a subjective emotion—an inner feeling rather than an outer relationship. We have been duped into thinking that cohabitation, marriage and divorce is primarily for and about adult happiness. We evaluate our relationship primarily according to how well it satisfies my own personal need (Cherlin 1992:71).

In a recent statement by the Catholic Bishops of Pennsylvania, they said sex is intensely private and personal, but it also has deep moral and social dimensions. Sex works as a primary bonding agent in families and the family is the building block of society. Sexual rights and wrongs influence the health and happiness of individuals, families, and neighborhoods. That's why sexual behavior has always been the subject of much civil law. The Church, of course, wishes to safeguard the family and society. But, more than that, the Church wishes to safeguard your relationship with your future spouse and with God. Sex is the act that seals and renews the couple's marriage covenant before God. Sexual sins, then, are not just between a man and a woman, but also between the couple and God. And that's the Church's responsibility. Sex is not simply a private matter. If it's between you and God, it's between you and the Church. You need to ask yourself, "When do I stop being a Christian? When I close the bedroom door? When does my relationship with God cease to matter?"

Appendix

Myth # 13:

What we do with our own bodies does not affect our relationship with each other or our spiritual relationship with God.

Again, the Catholic Bishops of Pennsylvania offer good advice: the gift of your body in sexual intercourse is a profound symbol of the giving of your whole self. In making love, the husband and wife are saying to one another in "body language" what they said to each other at the altar on their wedding day: "I am yours, for life!" God created sex to be physically pleasurable and emotionally fulfilling. But it is even greater than all that. It is, above all, the deepest sign of the complete gift of self that a husband and wife pledge to each other. This mutual gift empowers the couple to become co-creators with God in giving life to a new person, a baby. According to God's design, the gift of sexual union has two primary purposes: strengthening married love and sharing that love with children.

The only place where this total self-giving between a man and a woman is to take place is in marriage. It is the only place where children can be raised with the secure, committed love of a mother and a father. Therefore, sexual intimacy belongs only in marriage. Outside of marriage, sex is a lie. The action says, "I give you my whole self." But the man and woman are really holding back their commitment, their fertility, and their relationship with God. Before giving your body to another person, you need to give your whole life, and you need to receive your spouse's whole life in return—and that can only happen in marriage.

Myth # 14:

We can have sex together and not become involved, even on an emotional Level.

Dr. Neil Clark Warren of eHarmony, who has heard this numerous times says, "we know from our own studies that sexual involvement prior to a committed relationship of two persons who have vowed to remain faithful to each other for a lifetime always turns out to be problematical. When you get sexually involved with another, you become highly dependent on them. You become deeply involved at the most profound levels of your being. It is as though your psyche, your soul, your body, becomes totally interrelated with the other person's psyche, soul, and body, such that the two of you really are bonded on the most fundamental level possible." As soon as there is sexual involvement before marriage, the decision to get married becomes a foregone conclusion. "In other words, the sexual bonding caused them to assume that the decision about getting married had already been made. I believe that sexual bonding often takes place far before intercourse," says Dr. Warren.

> *"The monstrosity of sexual intercourse outside marriage is that those who indulge in it are trying to isolate one kind of union (the sexual) from all the other kinds of union which were intended to go along with it and make up the total union. The Christian attitude does not mean that there is anything wrong about sexual pleasure, any more than the pleasure of eating. It means that you must not isolate that pleasure and try to get it by itself, any more than you ought to try to get the pleasures of taste without swallowing and digesting, by chewing things and spitting them out again."*
>
> C. S. Lewis, *Mere Christianity*

From the Web site:
All About Cohabiting Before Marriage
Used by permission
Note: The host for this Web site has been shut down.
    A current Web address for this article is unknown.

Appendix

NOTES

Appendix

NOTES

Appendix

NOTES

Appendix

NOTES

Appendix

NOTES

Made in the USA
Monee, IL
21 January 2024

51512300R00098